# Taiwan's Economic Role in East Asia

# Significant Issues Series

SIGNIFICANT ISSUES SERIES papers are written for and published by the Center for Strategic and International Studies.

| | |
|---|---|
| Series Editors: | David M. Abshire |
| | Douglas M. Johnston |
| Director of Studies: | Erik R. Peterson |
| Director of Publications: | Nancy B. Eddy |
| Managing Editor: | Roberta L. Howard |
| Associate Editor: | Yoma Ullman |
| Editorial Assistant: | Kathleen M. McTigue |

❖    ❖    ❖

**The Center for Strategic and International Studies (CSIS),** founded in 1962, is an independent, tax-exempt, public policy research institution based in Washington, D.C. The mission of the Center is to advance the understanding of emerging world issues in the areas of international economics, politics, security, and business. It does so by providing a strategic perspective to decision makers that is integrative in nature, international in scope, anticipatory in its timing, and bipartisan in its approach. The Center's commitment is to serve the common interests and values of the United States and other countries around the world that support representative government and the rule of law.

CSIS, as a public policy research institution, does not take specific policy positions. Accordingly, all views, positions, and conclusions expressed in this publication should be understood to be solely those of the author.

The Center for Strategic and International Studies
1800 K Street, N.W.
Washington, D.C.   20006
Telephone: (202) 887-0200
Fax: (202) 775-3199

East Asia Economic and Financial Outlook
Gerrit W. Gong and Erik R. Peterson, Series Editors

# Taiwan's Economic Role in East Asia

Chi Schive

**THE CENTER FOR STRATEGIC & INTERNATIONAL STUDIES**
**Washington, D.C.**

Cover design by Hasten Design Studio.

Significant Issues Series, Volume XVII, Number 1
© 1995 by The Center for Strategic and International Studies
Washington, D.C.  20006
Printed on recycled paper in the United States of America

99   98   97   96   95          5   4   3   2   1

ISSN 0736-7136
ISBN 0-89206-319-X

**Library of Congress Cataloging-in-Publication Data**

Hsueh, Ch'i.
    Taiwan's economic role in East Asia / by Chi Schive ;
foreword by Gerrit W. Gong and Erik R. Peterson.
        p.  cm. — (Significant issues series, ISSN 0736-7136 ; v. 17, no. 1)
(East Asia economic and financial outlook)
Includes bibliographical references.
ISBN 0-89206-319-X
    1. Taiwan—Economic conditions—1975-   2. Taiwan—Foreign
economic relations.   3. Pacific Area—Foreign economic relations.
4. Pacific Area cooperation.   I. Title.   II. Series.   III. Series: Significant
issues series.   East Asia economic and financial outlook.
HC430.5.H784  1995
337.5124'9—dc20                                                                                    95-2644
                                                          CIP

# Contents

# Tables

# Charts

# East Asia Economic and Financial Outlook: Introduction to the Series

No doubt when future historians survey the topography of the late twentieth century, they will focus on the burst of economic activity that took place in East Asia. They will have good reason.

In a short time, many East Asian players have transformed their economic and financial systems into modern, dynamic structures generating high levels of growth and prosperity. They have propelled Asia as a region into real gross-domestic-product growth levels at or above 6.5 percent for the past two decades. They have transformed the region into one of the most competitive targets for foreign capital inflows. And they are now poised to carry forward this momentum into the third millennium.

These advances, as impressive as they are when expressed in macroeconomic terms, are all the more significant when translated into everyday life. Economic landscapes are changing fundamentally, and so too are the welfares of the populations. The new prosperity in the region is changing social patterns, generating new attitudes, and creating higher expectations. Furthermore, the change in economic and financial linkages between the East Asian economies—together with the expanded linkages between their populations—has been equally significant.

It should be stressed that this explosion of economic activity in East Asia is not the byproduct of a single driving factor such as the increase in world oil prices in the 1970s and its effect on oil-exporting states. Instead, it is being achieved through a variety of policy reorientations undertaken in significantly different economic and political structures with equally different factor endowments.

As a result, the constellation of economic, financial, political, and social changes that have culminated in the "East Asian miracle" is highly complex. While the region shares the common denominator of comparatively high levels of growth and export-driven expansion, the differences among its economies and political systems are profound. Each has its own staging point—and its own perceptions about the role its economy will play in the next century.

In thinking about the economic and financial dynamics of East Asia and the position the region is assuming in the world economy, we wanted to explore an array of economy-specific perceptions guiding policymakers in the region. A central question arises: To what extent do the plans that policymakers have for positioning their economies for the next century coincide, and to what extent do they collide?

This is the rationale for the *East Asia Economic and Financial Outlook* series published by the Asian Studies Program of the Center for Strategic and International Studies (CSIS). The series will present the insights of prominent East Asian analysts and draw conclusions about complementarities or divergences that may exist. Those insights, in turn, will serve in the aggregate as the basis for a richer, cross-cutting assessment of how the region will continue to develop and the role it can be expected to play in the quickly changing global economic and financial system.

At issue is the matrix of economy-specific considerations that characterize the region. What are the respective development strategies? Are they grounded in regionalism or globalism? How will those strategies be achieved? What additional reforms of the economic and financial systems are necessary? What comparative advantages are the economies seeking to establish as they move into the next century? These are a few of the key questions we have asked each author to address.

We begin the series with three separate analyses of "greater China," representing perspectives from Taiwan, Hong Kong, and the People's Republic of China. Such analysis must, by definition, be central to a broader regional assessment owing to the size of—and growth in—what has been referred to as the "Chinese economic area." Moreover, the ongoing political and economic redefinition of China—including the issues of succession and economic reform in Beijing, the realignment of political and economic forces in Taiwan, and the reversion of Hong Kong on July 1, 1997—suggests the importance of beginning our regional appraisal from these perspectives.

The series will include assessments of other key East Asian economies as well. With each volume, we hope to build a clearer picture of the regional contours and forces in the region that are shaping the twenty-first century economy in East Asia.

This series reflects the research and focus at CSIS on changes in the international economic and financial system. The Center has launched a number of initiatives covering a gamut of international financial issues, starting at home with an assessment of the U.S. regulatory system governing capital markets. Under the guidance of William A. Schreyer, chairman of the CSIS Board of Trustees' Executive Committee and chairman emeritus of Merrill Lynch & Company, Inc., CSIS has also been tracking global financial contingencies involving individual countries, regions, and transnational issues. Moreover, under the auspices of Maurice R. Greenberg, vice chairman of the CSIS Board of Trustees and chairman of the American International Group, Inc., CSIS is establishing a high-level international finance group that will convene regularly in New York.

We wish to thank several individuals who are contributing to this series. First, we express our deep appreciation to the authors for their analyses. Second, we acknowledge Keith W. Eirinberg, Chi J. Leng, Mary Marik, and Karen Wong of the CSIS Asian Studies Program; their commitment to this project reflects their competence and dedication. Finally, our appreciation goes to Nancy B. Eddy and Roberta L. Howard of the CSIS Publications Office for their important contributions to the production of these monographs.

GERRIT W. GONG
Freeman Chair in China Studies and
Director of Asian Studies, CSIS

ERIK R. PETERSON
Vice President and Director of Studies, CSIS
April 1995

# About the Author

Chi Schive is vice chairman of the Council for Economic Planning and Development of the Executive Yuan in Taipei and, concurrently, professor, chairperson, and director of the department of economics, National Taiwan University, Taipei. He is also a member of the National Income Committee, Directorate General of the Budget, Accounting, and Statistics in Taipei.

Dr. Schive received his Ph.D. and M.A. in economics from Case Western Reserve University, Cleveland, Ohio, and an additional M.A. from National Taiwan University. He has taught at Ohio University and was dean of the college of management at National Central University in Taipei. Dr. Schive has also been a visiting scholar at the Hoover Institute, at the Harvard-Yenching Institute, and at the East-West Center and a visiting professor at the Free University in Berlin.

Dr. Schive has contributed to many books on the economic development of Taiwan and the region, especially in the areas of industrial and trade development, technology transfer, foreign direct investment, and regional economic integration. He is the author of *The Foreign Factor: The Multinational's Contribution to the Economic Modernization of the Republic of China* (Hoover Institution Press, 1990).

# Foreword

The remarkable dynamism that has characterized East Asia over recent years has transformed not only the economic and financial contours of the region but also the topography of the global economic and financial system. The changes have been so profound that future historians may regard the "quiet revolution" that has taken place in East Asia as one of the seminal events of our times.

A number of analysts have looked closely at the reasons for the economic boom in East Asia. But what is all too often overshadowed in those assessments is the degree to which the economic players in the region share a common vision of the future.

The *East Asia Economic and Financial Outlook* series of studies addresses that critical issue. By offering differing perceptions by prominent authors on the outlook for East Asia, the series provides a new and important level of analysis. It will be useful to anyone committed to understanding how the region will develop through the end of the century and beyond.

WILLIAM A. SCHREYER
Chairman Emeritus, Merrill Lynch & Company, Inc., and
Chairman, Executive Committee, CSIS Board of Trustees

# 1

# Introduction

In the mid-1980s, Taiwan's economy reached a crucial stage. Taiwan had been registering impressive achievements in export promotion, industrialization, and income growth. Further advancement, however, seemed likely to take the economy on a downward slope. Meanwhile, great global changes were transpiring, although few could foresee the emergence of a new order amid the collapse, failure, and chaotic reorganization of the world's international political, financial, and trade arenas. As the world has adjusted to changing circumstances, Taiwan's economy has, painfully yet willingly, undergone a sooner-than-expected metamorphosis, with impetus from both external and internal shocks.

A significant economic power in the Asia-Pacific region, Taiwan is increasingly integrated with the world and the region. Its trade within East Asia and the Western Pacific has expanded much more rapidly than intraregional trade as a whole (chart 1.1). Moreover, as one of the top investors in East Asian economies, Taiwan has invested even more heavily in the region since the mid-1980s.

What is the world context within which Taiwan is reshaping its economy? What crucial forces can Taiwan develop into economic opportunities? What key interacting trends will determine the future of Taiwan's economy and those of its neighbors? How is Taiwan preparing itself to compete in the regional economy? How is Taiwan developing its new niche to survive world competition?

This monograph proposes to explore these questions by tracing the interaction of key elements in Taiwan's financial and business policies, both domestic and regional, beginning with the dynamic economic changes in East Asia. Chapter 2 discusses the surfacing new world economic order and the role of East Asia in the global economy. Chapters 3 and 4 spell out Taiwan's internal restructuring process, the development of external

**Chart 1.1**
**Indexes of Regional Trade Integration in NAFTA,**
**European Union, East Asia/Western Pacific, and Taiwan**

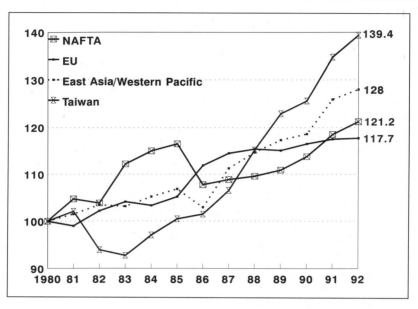

*Sources:*   International Monetary Fund, *Direction of Trade Statistics Yearbook,* various issues; Ministry of Finance, Taipei, *Monthly Statistics of Exports and Imports, Taiwan Area, The Republic of China,* various issues.

Notes:   The *index of regional trade integration* is defined as the ratio of intraregional trade to the region's total trade, based on 1980=100.
    The *index for Taiwan* is defined as the ratio of Taiwan's intraregional trade within East Asia/Western Pacific to the region's total trade, based on 1980=100.
    *NAFTA* refers to the economies of the United States, Canada, and Mexico.
    *European Union (EU)* refers to Germany, France, the United Kingdom, Italy, Spain, Portugal, Ireland, Belgium, the Netherlands, Luxembourg, Denmark, and Greece.
    *East Asia/Western Pacific* refers to Japan, South Korea, Taiwan, Singapore, Hong Kong, Thailand, Malaysia, Indonesia, the Philippines, Australia, New Zealand, and mainland China.

economic relations, and the interactions between the two. Chapter 5 focuses on Taiwan's economic relations with mainland China and their complementarity and competition. Chapters 6 and 7 touch on Taiwan's opportunities to play an important role in the Asia-Pacific region, particularly as a regional operations center. Chapter 8 offers a summation and projection of Taiwan's future economic role in the region.

# 2

# The New Order in East Asia

The past few years have witnessed remarkable changes: the fall of the Berlin Wall, the end of the cold war, and the collapse of Communist regimes in Eastern Europe.

As the world enters a great age of restructuring and evolution, economic issues have largely replaced military confrontation in shaping the new order. This economic focus will be carried even farther with the establishment of the World Trade Organization (WTO), which will set rules to facilitate global trade and give businesses the means by which to go global. Accordingly, this section considers the new world trade order, regionalization, the rise of East Asia, globalization, and glasnost and perestroika.

## The New World Trade Order

Since the mid-1980s, several forces have shaped the world economy. First, the successful conclusion of the Uruguay Round of the General Agreement on Tariffs and Trade (GATT) has given birth to the WTO, which is weaving a more open world trade fabric. Second, the formation of regional blocs has accelerated, and some regional communities have been transformed into tighter, more defensive blocs. Third, the Asia-Pacific region has become part of the world's economic center of gravity. Fourth, more and more enterprises are going global. And, fifth, Communist countries are adapting themselves to market economics.

After seven years of numerous meetings and negotiations, the Uruguay Round talks were concluded on December 15, 1993. Their goal was the reduction of trade and investment barriers and the extension of current GATT rules on the General Agreement on Trade in Services (GATS) under the WTO. Implementation of the new rules will liberalize the world trade framework, intensify business competition, and open individual economies.

Global trade, investment, and other economic practices will be fashioned by the following four developments:

- *A new multilateral trade organization will redefine the global trade order.*   The WTO took effect on January 1, 1995, replacing the GATT, the informal world trade body that is due to lapse on December 31, 1995. The formal WTO organization is expected to strengthen the implementation and management of trade agreements and to advance world trade liberalization.
- *More areas will be covered by trade rules.*   Areas covered by GATT rules have been greatly expanded following the Uruguay Round. In addition to general merchandise, all areas not governed by GATT rules, including textiles, agriculture, services, investment, and intellectual property rights, have been negotiated.
- *Tariffs will be reduced for all goods.*   Tariffs on industrial products will be reduced by one-third. For some products, such as medicine, construction materials, medical equipment, paper, and steel, tariffs will be completely eliminated. Tariffs on agricultural products will be reduced by an average of 36 percent in 6 years in the industrial countries and by 24 percent in 10 years in the developing countries. The tariffication of nontariff barriers on agricultural products will be introduced and tariff rates will be subsequently reduced.
- *Dispute settlement will be strengthened.*   The Uruguay Round agreement includes a special memorandum to speed up the dispute settlement procedure and improve its effectiveness. As a result, a department will be set up under the WTO to take responsibility for dispute settlement and to enhance the settlement mechanism.

## Regionalization

As the cold war faded, the basis of international rivalry switched from arms to economic competition. Europe, North America, and Asia and the Pacific, by means of interregional and intraregional cooperation and competition, are emerging as the three great pillars of the world economy in an era of liberalized trade.

In the 1980s, regional economic planners drafted plans for regional economic integration. In the early 1990s, relevant legislation was completed and brought agreements and treaties into effect throughout the world: first came the European Union (EU), defined by the Treaty of Maastricht; then North America was united by the North American Free Trade Agreement (NAFTA). Now the world is waiting to see how the dynamic Asia-Pacific region will move toward integration.

*European Union.* European economic unification began to gather speed in 1985, when planners proposed a white paper concerning the formation of the Single European Market. The market was officially formed in January 1993, and in November 1993 the Maastricht treaty was jointly signed. At the same time, the European Community (EC) was reorganized into the EU, which set a six-year schedule for economic and monetary unification. In January 1994, the Single European Market was extended to the European Free Trade Association (EFTA) countries; in a combined European Economic Area (EEA), these countries collectively represent the world's largest free trade group, representing 17 member states with a combined population of 370 million and a combined gross domestic product (GDP) of $7 trillion.[1]

*North American Free Trade Area.* The Canada-U.S. free trade area was implemented in January 1989. With Mexico's inclusion on January 1, 1994, North America became the world's second largest free trade area. The three countries, which make up a huge market of more than 300 million consumers and have a collective GDP of more than $6 trillion, have scheduled a gradual phase-out of tariffs and nontariff barriers among contracting members.

*Economic Integration in Asia and the Pacific.* Although the Asia-Pacific region has been growing rapidly for the past quarter century, economic integration has quickened only in the past 10 years. The primary cause is the growth of foreign investment. Both Japan and Asia's newly industrializing economies (NIEs)[2] have rapidly expanded their investment in the region, partly in response to the threat posed by economic integration in Europe and North America.

The countries of the Association of Southeast Asian Nations (ASEAN)[3] have led in organizing the region's economic integration at the governmental level; at the end of 1992, they announced the concept of an ASEAN Free Trade Area (AFTA).

Other organizations have also been upgraded and strengthened to improve Asia-Pacific economic cooperation: for example, the Asia-Pacific Economic Cooperation (APEC) forum expanded from 12 to 18 economies and held unprecedented Asia-Pacific summits in Seattle in November 1993 and in Jakarta a year later.

Driven by market forces, diversity in resource endowments, developments in technology, degree of industrialization, and market scale, countries in the region have created formal and informal subregional groupings in areas such as the Sea of Japan, the triangle linking Singapore, Malaysia, and Indonesia, and the triangle linking Hong Kong, Taiwan, and the southeast coast of the Chinese mainland. Industrial integration and specialization among countries in the region have become more visible and have generated significant benefits.

A far more active intraregional flow of capital, technology, and human resources will challenge the conventional wisdom focusing on intercountry commodity flows. A similar trend may develop at the company level: in international markets, countries may form strategic alliances instead of pursuing head-to-head competition. Whether cooperation or competition will become the dominant force in shaping the world economic order is a crucial question.

## East Asia on the Rise

Europe and North America are the largest and second-largest global markets. Although Asia as a whole has led global economic growth by industrializing according to the flying-geese pattern, the recessions that have overshadowed the world's two largest economic powers since the late 1980s have likewise affected Asia. Many predict that the Pacific Rim economies will collectively become the largest global market in the distant future; they are already in third place.

*Fastest Growth.* According to Wharton Econometric Forecasting Associates (WEFA), the economies of East Asian developing countries, which include the NIEs, ASEAN, and mainland China, grew on average 7.5 percent each year between 1990 and 1993, much higher than Japan's 2.6 percent, the United States' 1.5 percent, and the EU's 1.2 percent. In 1993, developing Asia continued to outperform the industrial countries and registered a combined growth of 8.3 percent. Led by Japan, the NIEs have followed a fast growth track, and ASEAN also has begun its journey toward development and industrialization. China has now joined them as a third wave. Even Vietnam is sometimes mentioned as a new addition to the flying-geese pattern.

***An Expanding Market.***   Asia-Pacific prosperity was built on international trade with the developed countries, particularly the United States. Increasing domestic demand in the United States has driven Asian export growth over the past two or three decades. Today, however, East Asian growth no longer needs to depend on exports to developed countries as much as it did in the past. Currently, much Asian trade is taking place within the region itself.

In 1986, for example, East Asian developing countries shipped 60.5 percent of their exports to the United States, Japan, and the EC and only 29.4 percent to Asian developing countries. By 1992, the developed countries' share had declined to 46.3 percent while Asian developing countries had increased their share to 40.6 percent. International Monetary Fund (IMF) statistics show that Asian developing countries are now the largest market for East Asian products.[4]

East Asian developing countries are also an expanding market for industrial countries: between 1986 and 1992, their share of industrial countries' exports grew from 7.6 percent to 10.4 percent.

Finally, the Asian NIEs have become a very significant market for their neighbors. In 1992, they absorbed about half of mainland China's exports and more than one-fifth of the total exports of the ASEAN-4.[5] They also imported 21.4 percent of Japan's exports.

Although some argue that the bulk of intraregional trade is in components and semifinished materials for goods destined for developed countries, there is no doubt that the regional consumer market is expanding and becoming increasingly attractive. Rapid export expansion is boosting industrial growth and disposable incomes, creating a burgeoning consumer class in the region. In addition, domestic investment is expanding significantly because rapid development creates an explosive need for infrastructure, making the region an alluring market for capital.

***Foreign Direct Investment.***   Overseas investment has propelled Asia's spectacular growth. From 1987 to 1991, foreign direct investment (FDI) in the ASEAN countries increased more than fivefold, and in mainland China it almost doubled.[6] FDI brings with it more advanced or more appropriate technologies, better equipment, and more efficient management, and it promotes rapid economic progress in the host country.

Japan and the Asian NIEs, Taiwan in particular, have invested heavily in the Asian-Pacific region recently. The NIEs, hoping to maintain their global cost-competitiveness, are seeking cheaper manufacturing locations in such places as the ASEAN-4, mainland China, and Vietnam. Japan and Taiwan have also boosted their investment in Asia to hedge against what they perceive as the possibility of European and North American protectionism and to diversify their export markets in general.

**Intraregional Trade.**   Intraregional investment has contributed to the rapid expansion of intraregional trade and has reduced East Asia's export dependency on developed country markets. The new status of the NIEs as a significant market for other Asian countries has reduced the region's dependence on the economies of the Group of 7 (G-7),[7] aided regional specialization, and maintained economic vibrancy in developing Asia despite economic stagnancy in Europe, North America, and Japan. This is certainly a new trend.

Japan is an important supplier of intermediate goods to the NIEs and the ASEAN countries but, by supplying more intermediates to other NIEs in the region and to the ASEAN-4, the NIEs are now playing a role similar to that of Japan. Trade triangles are being formed not only with Japan as the supplier of intermediates but also with a number of other regional economies.

**East Asia and the Industrial Countries.**   Facing rising wages, union pressures, and stagnant productivity in their domestic economies, the industrial countries used to invest in East Asia to take advantage of low labor costs. And the region still offers ample supplies of lower-cost labor. In addition, as Asian countries emerge with greater purchasing power, technological expertise, and convenient access to intermediate goods, they are also ready to consume an increasing share of finished products, reinforcing their attractiveness to industrial country manufacturers as investment locations.

**Japan's Role.**   Japan is Asia's largest economic power, and its success has made it a model for other Asian countries. Since the mid-1980s, the strong yen has caused Japanese companies to increase overseas investment. Facing trade pressures and slower growth in Europe and North America, Japan has been cashing in on its Asian neighbors' need for sophisticated Japanese capital goods and components to produce their own exports. Taking advantage of geographical proximity and making use of its plentiful financial and technological resources, Japan has established an intraregional division of labor as well as a production network. East Asian economies have become not only important consumer markets for Japanese products but also providers of low-cost supplies to Japan.

For a long time, however, Japan has exported more to the region than it has imported from it. Although it is running a large trade surplus with other economies in the region, Japan has not offered its neighbors easier access to its own market. According to IMF data, Japan's trade surplus with Asian developing countries grew from $15.3 billion to $53.1 billion from 1987 to 1993. This surplus surpassed Japan's surpluses with the EC and with the United States.

Other Asian countries have had difficulties reducing their deficits with Japan because their industries depend heavily on Japanese supplies of industrial raw materials, components, and capital goods. Although these countries are seeking to upgrade their industries in the hope of freeing themselves from Japanese dominance in conventional sectors, their dependence on Japanese technology and high-tech intermediates is even greater in the newly developed sectors. Asian countries could form a regional bloc excluding Japan, but the trade imbalance with Japan will show little improvement until the Japanese market becomes more accessible to its Asian neighbors.

The experience of the Japanese invasion during World War II has made some Asian countries distrustful of Japan's increasing regional economic role. A powerful yen bloc is unlikely to form despite Japan's overall influence in Asia. Rather, many of Japan's neighbors seek to acquire capital and technology from and expand economic ties with Europe and North America to counterbalance growing Japanese clout in the East Asian economy.

## Globalization

In the information age, companies can pursue business opportunities abroad through modern communications technologies. Many multinational enterprises constantly expand their businesses beyond their own national boundaries and plan for increasing global or regional organization, production facilities, resource reallocation, and other related businesses.

A look at global FDI trends confirms the rapid expansion of global operations and the proliferation of multinational corporations. United Nations (UN) statistics show that global FDI has mounted quickly since the late 1980s: world trade expanded 6 percent in volume annually between 1986 and 1990, but FDI grew 24 percent annually in the same period. In contrast, during the early 1980s, FDI grew only 4 percent each year. Trade-oriented investment dominates current capital movements.

Multinational corporations have gained importance in world economic activities. According to the UN, total sales of multinationals amounted to $5.5 trillion in 1991. This represents a quarter of the world's GDP and far exceeds the $4 trillion in global trade in goods and services that year. In some cases, a single multinational corporation's annual turnover has surpassed the GDP of an entire country.

In earlier years, multinational corporations targeted industrial countries for investment. Fast growth, especially in East Asia, has attracted multinational investment to developing countries. The UN has estimated that between 1986 and 1990 only 17 percent of global FDI went to developing countries. By 1992,however, that figure had risen to 32 percent. East Asia has absorbed about half the FDI in the developing world in recent years, its share of total FDI growing from 9 percent in the late 1980s to 17 percent in 1993.

In the past, multinational corporations also invested in basic industries. More recently, they have targeted technology-intensive manufacturing and service sectors. Investment in the service sector increased rapidly in the 1980s, resulting in the concentration of more than 50 percent of industrial country FDI in that sector in 1990. In developing countries, however, FDI from industrial countries has remained concentrated in manufacturing.

## Glasnost and Perestroika

Fundamental and comprehensive political and economic reform signified the rebirth of the former Soviet bloc after the dismantling of the Warsaw Treaty Organization and the Council for Mutual Economic Assistance (COMECON) in 1991. Before their market-oriented reforms, however, these countries faced serious transition difficulties and incurred sharp short-term reform costs. The breakdown of the old system has led to a high degree of uncertainty and has disrupted existing patterns of economic practices, difficulties that have been greatly magnified by a series of economic "shocks" imposed both internally and externally. Yet, despite declining production and high inflation among eastern and central European countries, democratization and economic restructuring have continued throughout the region.

Other socialist states are reorienting from centrally planned to market-oriented economies and from isolation to opening. For example, mainland China and Vietnam have implemented a wide range of reforms—opening their domestic economies to the rest of the world, promoting external economic relations, and inviting foreign investment—to achieve rapid economic development. The progress of the reforms has been promising, and the outlook for these countries is bright.

The destruction of the wall separating East and West has made available a workforce willing to form a new global production network; its impact on the world economy and the international division of labor will be enormous and profound.

# 3

# Taiwan's Great Transition in the 1980s

A look back at Taiwan's development experience over more than four decades reveals that each stage of Taiwan's economic development has had an unique set of conditions and has been distinguished by a specific policy. In the 1950s, the focus was on import substitution to achieve self-sufficiency; in the 1960s, the emphasis shifted to the active promotion of exports to support industrial expansion and boost foreign reserves; and in the 1970s, export promotion continued and was supplemented by a second phase of import substitution of upstream industries.

In the 1980s, the Taiwan economy was confronted by two related phenomena: mounting trade surpluses and escalating excess savings. This situation was the converse of Taiwan's predicament in the early postwar years when it suffered from inadequate domestic production, insufficient investment capital, current account deficits, and huge balance-of-payments deficits.

During this period, the value of the New Taiwan dollar (NT dollar) came under tremendous upward pressure, and its sharp appreciation eroded Taiwan's international competitiveness. Restructuring forged Taiwan's new era of economic progress and its new role in the Asia-Pacific region and was achieved by dealing with both macroeconomic imbalances and microeconomic adjustments.

## Macroeconomic Imbalances

During the 1980s, Taiwan's trade surplus multiplied as exports grew much faster than imports. The exports/GNP ratio remained at about 52 percent between 1980 and 1983 and increased to 56 percent in 1986 and 1987, while the imports/ GNP ratio declined steadily until 1987 (table 3.1). Between 1982 and 1986, the average annual growth rate for exports of goods and services was 13.6 percent, while that of imports was only 4.5 percent, one-third of that figure.

Taiwan's 1986 merchandise trade surplus of $15.6 billion was much lower than Japan's ($83.2 billion) and West Germany's ($52.5 billion). But as a percentage of GNP—19.3 percent—it was unparalleled among non-oil producing countries. If the surplus in services trade is included, the trade surplus amounted to 22.1 percent of GNP, far greater than the surpluses of Japan and Germany, which were both less than 5 percent of GNP. The mounting trade surplus exerted tremendous upward pressure on the NT dollar. On September 22, 1985, the Group of 5 (G-5) nations[8] intervened to devalue the U.S. dollar, and the NT dollar appreciated sharply. By the end of 1987, the NT dollar had appreciated 42 percent against the U.S. dollar, the highest rate among Asia's major currencies during this period.

Except for controls on inward remittances, foreign exchange controls in Taiwan were removed in July 1987, and Taiwan's Central Bank of China had to continue to absorb foreign exchange to maintain the stability of the foreign exchange market. At the end of 1987, the foreign exchange reserves of the central bank exceeded $77 billion, up from $9 billion five years earlier. Despite various sterilization measures, the money supply grew at an annual rate of more than 20 percent during the 34 months from March 1986 to the end of 1988 and by more than 30 percent during 24 of those months. During the second half of 1988, the money supply grew about 30 percent and placed strong inflationary pressure on domestic prices.

The counterpart of the economy's huge external imbalances is its excess savings, which signify a shortfall of domestic demand. During the 1980s, Taiwan's GNP continued to expand while domestic demand slowed substantially. Between 1982 and 1986, nominal GNP rose 9.8 percent a year on average while domestic demand increased only 4.7 percent. This disparity implies a rapidly expanding excess of savings over investment; in fact, savings rose to 22.1 percent of GNP in 1986. Between 1981 and 1986, investment declined rapidly, from 30 percent to 17 percent of GNP, approaching its level in the 1950s.

In addition to allowing the NT dollar to appreciate substantially to reduce its trade surplus, the Taiwan government pursued the following liberalization policies:

- As noted above, it removed almost all foreign-exchange controls in June 1987 except for restrictions on inward remittances. Retention of these restrictions has prevented an influx of foreign hot money to Taiwan.

- It lowered import tariffs. Comprehensive tariff reduction brought the average nominal tariff rate down to half its previous level and the real import tariff rate (total customs duties/total imports) to 5.9 percent in 1990.
- It relaxed large-scale import restrictions. Most regulations restricting the issuance of import documents and the origin of imports were eliminated in May 1987. Only 1.5 percent of commodities on import manifests were banned, controlled, or delayed.
- It opened the domestic market for services to external competition. Fast food outlets, supermarkets, banks, insurance firms, leasing agencies, and marine shipping services of foreign concerns gained access to the domestic market. Foreign firms already in Taiwan were allowed to expand the scope of their operations.

## Microeconomic Adjustments

The rapid appreciation of the NT dollar forced labor costs, calculated in U.S. dollars, to rise at an extremely rapid rate. Although the unit labor cost remained relatively stable between 1981 and 1985, after the devaluation of the U.S. dollar in 1986 the unit labor cost index[9] sharply increased, recording the fastest rate of increase for all major industrialized economies. With 1982 as a base year, Taiwan's rising unit labor cost during the 1980s compared unfavorably with other manufacturing countries (table 3.2), and the international competitiveness of Taiwan's traded products appeared to be affected. Other factors being equal, this negative impact was largely due to exchange rate revaluation.

The weaker NT dollar had previously facilitated export expansion, and the export-oriented manufacturing sector accounted for a high share of Taiwan's GDP in the early and middle 1980s. Its share declined, however, from 39.7 percent in 1986 to 32.9 percent in 1992 because export growth slowed in response to currency revaluation. Prompted by rising labor costs and encouraged by the government's liberalization measures, Taiwan's manufacturers were quick to adjust to a lower share in GDP. They relocated production of the least competitive products by increasing overseas investment, accelerated automation, restructured exports away from labor-intensive goods, promoted the production of high value-added products, and employed inexpensive foreign labor.

*Automation.* Although the dynamic view of automation is linked to the concept of technological progress and the phenomenon of learning, the short-term static version of introducing automated techniques involves capital deepening and the substitution of labor. One measure of automation is the ratio of the number of machines with automatic control mechanisms relative to the total number of machines in use. In five industries—foods, textiles, plastic products, machinery, and electronics—there was a clear trend toward increased use of automatic machinery. Between 1982 and 1991, the food industry quickly attained a high degree of automation, while the four other industries showed varying degrees of achievement (see table 3.3).

Another measure is the value of automatic machinery per worker, which also displays a significant increasing trend between 1985 and 1991. Although both indicators show that automation accelerated after 1986 when the NT dollar began to appreciate sharply, simply looking at the two measures understates the actual extent of automation process. First, when a firm installs new automatic machinery, it may keep the old machinery in reserve rather than dispose of it. Thus, the total number of machines is overstated and the automatic machinery ratio dampened. Second, one piece of new automatic machinery may replace a larger number of conventional machines. Thus, the numbers alone completely ignore the issue of efficiency. For example, although the food industry increased its use of automatic machinery by only 13 percentage points from 1985 to 1987, its operational efficiency should have increased by more than that, because each new generation of machinery may perform better than the existing one. Third, industrial automation increases with the learning process. In the beginning it proceeds more slowly because most firms bring automatic machinery into their operations on a small-scale, trial basis. Firms install automatic machinery on a grander scale as the good results become more noticeable. Finally, the price of automation equipment declined during this period because of the strong NT dollar. As a result, the total value of automatic machinery per worker in real terms was higher than the figures indicate.

Between 1987 and 1991, Taiwan's manufacturing employment fell 16 percent, from 2.62 million to 2.20 million. The manufacturing production index, however, posted a 14 percent increase over the same period. Automation enabled manufacturers to increase production using less labor—implying a gain in labor productivity. The 56.3 percent growth of manufacturing output between 1981 and 1986 and the 28.8 percent growth between 1986 and 1991 indicate that labor productivity improvement was the major factor contributing to continued output growth.

*Quality Improvement.*    Another effective solution to the problem of decreasing competitiveness is to upgrade product quality rather than to lower prices. Between 1986 and 1989, the export price index in NT dollars displayed a declining trend, implying that Taiwan exporters lowered their prices without quality improvement. Between 1986 and 1990, however, the unit export price deflated by the export price in NT dollars revealed an increasing trend, pointing to quality improvement in Taiwan's export products.[10]

The bicycle industry, for example, seeking to protect its international market share against the appreciating NT dollar relative to the U.S. dollar, stepped up the development of new materials, new components, and new models to improve prices. One result was the development of a new material that could substitute for aluminum in bicycle production; mass use of the new material got under way in 1988. Also, by developing key components, Taiwan's bicycle industry was able to reduce its dependence on component imports and increase component exports at the same time. The effect was remarkable: the unit price jumped from U.S.$ 47.1 in 1986 to U.S.$ 119 in 1993.

*Composition of Merchandise Trade.*    Because labor-intensive export industries were affected significantly by rising labor costs, Taiwan manufacturers turned to labor-saving methods of production, shifting their labor-intensive production overseas and concentrating on capital- and technology-intensive products. In 1986, products with high labor intensity accounted for 47 percent of total exports. This share fell to 41 percent in 1990 and to 38.8 percent in 1993. During the same period, the export share of highly capital-intensive products increased from 22.9 percent in 1986 to 32 percent in 1993. The share of highly technology-intensive products also increased, from 18.4 percent in 1986 to 29.5 percent in 1992 (table 3.4). Labor-intensive consumer nondurable goods, once Taiwan's most important export products, declined among Taiwan's total exports, contracting from 35.6 percent in 1986 to 18.1 percent in 1993 (table 3.5).

The relocation of production overseas has boosted exports of machinery and intermediate goods. In 1986, as shown in table 3.5, machinery accounted for 10.9 percent of total exports, while intermediate goods B made up 26.1 percent. By 1990, these figures had risen to 16.3 percent and 35.0 percent respectively. In 1993, the export share of machinery was 17.5 percent, suggesting a stabilizing growth of initial investments, and the share of intermediate goods B was 37.8 percent.

# 4

# Taiwan's Economic Restructuring and Regional Integration

In the 1980s, Taiwan turned from being a cash-poor capital importer to a cash-rich capital source. By the late 1980s, outward investment was playing a major role in the restructuring of Taiwan's economy while it fostered extensive links with the rest of the Asia-Pacific region through outward investment, intraregional trade, and technological exchanges.

## Outward Investment

Taiwanese entrepreneurs have been attracted to opportunities in Southeast Asian countries and mainland China since 1986.[11] Besides economic considerations, two additional factors influence Taiwan's outward investment in these areas: cultural similarities, and the high degree of complementarity between Taiwan and the other Asian economies. Because Taiwan now lacks abundant land, natural resources, and low-skilled labor, it must export capital, skilled manpower, well-rounded industrial production systems, and marketing networks to neighboring Southeast Asian countries to capitalize on their natural resources and abundant labor force as well as markets (table 4.1). Efforts by Southeast Asian governments to attract Taiwanese capital have also been conducive to the rapid expansion of Taiwanese offshore investment.

Taiwan's government-approved outward investment totaled only $7.5 million in the 1960s and $51.7 million in the 1970s. Between 1986 and 1990, however, it almost doubled every year, increasing from $56.9 million to $1,552 million (table 4.2).

Data from host countries indicate investment levels may have actually been even higher; the disparity is more than 100 times in some cases. For instance, although Taiwan's officially approved investment to Indonesia totaled $1.9 million in 1988, Indonesian statistics record $913 million. Host country data also indicate that by the end of 1993, Taiwan was Vietnam's largest foreign investor; Taiwan ranked second in Malaysia, third in Indonesia, fourth in Thailand, and fifth in the Philippines. Host country data indicate Taiwan's investment in Southeast Asia as a whole totaled $16.1 billion between 1959 and 1993. During this period Taiwan-based capital totaling $1.5 billion poured into Vietnam, $5.9 billion to Malaysia, $3.6 billion to Indonesia, $4.5 billion to Thailand, and $442 million to the Philippines (tables 4.3, 4.4, and 4.5).

As mainland China became more open to capitalism, with the warming of its cross-strait relationship with Taiwan since the late 1980s, and as Southeast Asian governments gradually reduced their incentive provisions, investment in mainland China looked more profitable to Taiwan investors and had expanded more rapidly. The substitution effect was dramatic in 1992. Data from both host governments and Taiwan's Investment Commission, Ministry of Economic Affairs, show a remarkable decline in Taiwan's outward investment in that year, while Taiwan's investment in mainland China, tabulated by the Investment Commission as "indirect" rather than "outward" investment, increased almost fourfold (tables 4.2 and 4.3). Nevertheless, Taiwan's total outward direct investment will continue to grow, but a moderate growth rate is expected.

Some of Taiwan's investment has likely been made through Hong Kong because, historically, Hong Kong has been an important financial center in the Asia-Pacific region. These investments, however, are covered in the records of neither Taiwan nor the host countries.

Traditional manufacturing industries such as textiles, electronics and electrical appliances, paper products and printing, chemical products, and metal products and non-metallic products receive most of Taiwan's overseas investment in Southeast Asian economies, excluding Hong Kong and Singapore. Most of Taiwan's investment in Hong Kong and Singapore has been in services such as trade, banking and insurance, and wholesale and retail (table 4.6).

The surge in Taiwan's investment in Southeast Asia and mainland China should not be interpreted as the result of government policy to concentrate only in these areas (table 4.7). Approved investment data show that the United States used to be the most attractive country for Taiwan investors, accounting for 72.6 percent of Taiwan's total outward investment from 1980 to 1986. From 1987 to 1991, however, the U.S. share fell to 32 percent despite investments by large Taiwan-based companies in many well-known projects in the United States, such as those initiated by Formosa Plastic Group and Acer. In 1993, the United States was still the second most important destination for Taiwan's approved outbound investment, but it accounted for only 11.5 percent of the total, following mainland China's 47 percent. Malaysia ranked third with 9.7 percent of total outbound investment; Hong Kong, fourth with 8.3 percent; and Thailand, fifth with 8.1 percent.

In Eastern Europe, including the former Soviet Union, newly opening markets created abundant opportunities for Taiwan's investors. Several Taiwan personal computer producers as well as traders have already responded to market signals. Although amounts remain modest, investment growth has been high. Taiwan's investors have been quick to adopt a global view in expediting planning for their upcoming operations.

Since the late 1980s, some have feared that massive offshore investment by local enterprises would exhaust Taiwan's economy. But, according to the Ministry of Economic Affairs (MOEA), most local companies that have invested overseas during the past seven years have also continued to invest in Taiwan. Rather than eroding Taiwan's industrial base, increasing foreign investment by Taiwan-based firms has been a first step in globalizing local enterprises. An MOEA survey showed that of the 4,056 manufacturers that have invested abroad, 59.6 percent continue to maintain their investments in Taiwan and 24.3 percent plan to expand local business operations.[12] The firms most likely to eliminate or reduce operations in Taiwan are manufacturers of ready-to-wear garments, leather, wood materials, and rubber; these types of productive activities are losing comparative advantage in Taiwan.

## Intraregional Trade

Taiwan's trade with its neighbors to the east and south has expanded rapidly since the second half of the 1980s due to Taiwan's growing investment in neighboring economies. The impact of outward investment on trade can be analyzed from two aspects: the composition of trade and the direction of trade (tables 4.8 and 4.9).

Since the late 1960s, the United States has been Taiwan's most important trading partner: it has been Taiwan's largest export market and its second largest source of imports (see tables 4.10 and 4.11). Taiwan's dependence on the U.S. market increased sharply in the first half of the 1980s: the U.S. share of Taiwan's exports increased from 34.1 percent in 1980 to 48.8 percent in 1984 and 48.1 percent in 1985. By 1990, however, a combination of falling exports to the United States and rising exports to ASEAN, the Asian NIEs, and mainland China (table 4.12), as well as to Europe, had pushed this figure down to 32.4 percent; it decreased further to 27.7 percent in 1993. In contrast, exports to Hong Kong accounted for 18.9 percent of Taiwan's total exports in 1992, more than double the export ratio of 6.9 percent in 1984. By the first half of 1994, the ASEAN-5—Indonesia, Malaysia, the Philippines, Singapore, and Thailand—were Taiwan's fourth largest export market, taking 11.1 percent of Taiwan's exports in that period; the United States, Hong Kong, and Japan ranked first, second, and third with 25.9 percent, 22.9 percent, and 10.7 percent respectively.

Taiwan's overseas investments have played a large role in this shift. Because many Taiwan firms have moved their factories overseas, Taiwan has become an important exporter of capital and intermediate goods to neighboring economies that, in turn, produce goods for the U.S. market (table 4.13).

At the company level, Taiwan's trade with ASEAN has displayed an increasingly cooperative relationship; as seen in table 4.14, the intra-industry trade coefficient indicates that industrial integration among these economies has expanded greatly. The coefficient suggests vast vertical integration—trade in finished or semifinished products within the industry—or horizontal integration when its value approaches 100 percent. Between 1985 and 1991, the figure for Taiwan-ASEAN intra-industry trade increased from 19.7 percent to 36.5 percent.

## Technological Exchanges

There is no question that Taiwan's investment has helped expand and upgrade the industrial sectors of host developing countries in the Asia-Pacific region.

First, Taiwan investors have helped those countries capitalize on their comparative advantages by creating jobs and export opportunities.

Second, because Taiwan's entrepreneurs send technology, engineers, and managers to host countries, Taiwan's investment can have longer-term impact on the technological development of those countries. A few figures give a picture of the potential impact. For example, between 1986 and 1993 royalty income received by Taiwan rose from $4 million to $332 million, the lion's share of which came from other developing countries in Asia (table 4.15). Travel data are another indicator of Taiwan's active involvement in technology transfer. In 1993, 87 percent of the 314,510 Taiwan nationals who traveled abroad for business purposes went to Hong Kong, Japan, South Korea, and ASEAN countries. And 77 percent of the 12,383 travelers to overseas conferences also headed for those countries (table 4.16). The number of technical cooperation contracts is a straightforward indicator of the diffusion of Taiwan's technology in the region. However, official statistics show only 62 reported cases of such projects between 1964 and 1993.[13] That figure is questionable, however, because of the size of Taiwan's investment and royalties received in the region.

Subsidiaries of Taiwan multinationals in host countries can upgrade their own product structure over time because they have access to the parent companies' deep pocket of experience, global marketing networks, and customer bases. In addition, the overall technological level in host countries can be improved through original equipment manufacturing, on-the-job training by Taiwan-based employers, and manufacturing, marketing, and service alliances, as well as by industrial espionage.

The government itself is also keen on promoting technological cooperation with other countries in the Asia-Pacific region. Many joint conferences between Taiwan and other Asia-Pacific economies have been held on trade, science and technology, investment, agriculture, and energy. Special technological assistance programs in manpower training, economic development research, and financial assistance have been offered to such countries as the Philippines, Vietnam, and Thailand.[14] In addition, trade associations in Taiwan have sponsored similar activities.

# 5

# Relations between the Two Sides across the Taiwan Strait

Over the past decade, the domestic and global circumstances of both Taiwan and mainland China have changed, transforming the relations between the two across the Taiwan Strait.

First, Taiwan's economy has undergone massive structural transformation since the late 1980s. Second, the mainland's opening, its rapid economic development, and the consequent influence of that development have become irreversible. In addition, global political and commercial situations have changed: the disintegration of the Soviet Union, which signaled the bankruptcy of communism and the end of the cold war, and the rise of globalization and regionalism have all taken place in the last decade.

Since the 1980s, economic liberalization and internationalization have dominated Taiwan's economic platform, while trade and investment links with the mainland have added a new dimension to Taiwan's development. With the thawing of tensions across the strait, cross-strait relations have evolved from alienation and confrontation to gradual reengagement through economic, cultural, academic, and athletic exchanges. Because of expanding cross-strait economic links, any discussion of Taiwan's economic future must take into account the position of the mainland.

The following briefly summarizes cross-strait developments since 1979 (see chart 5.1), including a chronological review, cross-strait trade, competition between Beijing and Taipei in major markets, Taiwan's investment in the mainland, and alternative scenarios for the future.

## Chronological Review

*1979–1983.* In 1979, the mainland government released a "letter to a Taiwan compatriot" that marked the start of a series of dramatic changes in the Communist government's Taiwan

**Chart 5.1**
**Recent Policy Changes regarding Cross-Strait Relations**

---

*Mainland China's Policy toward Economic Links with Taiwan*

**Jan 1979**   Issued "A letter to Taiwan compatriot" to call for immediate business, mail, and transportation links.

**May 1979**   Stipulated temporary rules governing trade development with Taiwan.

**March 1980**   Circulated an internal document of the Ministry of Commerce to specify national (tariff-waiving) treatment to Taiwan products, first purchase priority to Taiwan imports, and 20% discount on sales to Taiwan.

**May 1981**   Cancelled preferential tariff treatment to Taiwan products and the 20% discount privilege on sales to Taiwan except to Taiwan citizens making the purchase in the mainland.

**April 1983**   State Council announced three preferential measures to Taiwan investment in special economic zones and in Hainan.

**June 1985**   Set ban on imports of Taiwan consumer products. Concentrated imports from Taiwan through Fujian and Hainan. In October, lifted the ban on electrical appliances and textile products from Taiwan. In December, ordered that applications for Taiwan imports had to be approved by the mainland's unification departments.

**July 1987**   State Council announced that all trade with Taiwan had to be administered by economics and trade authorities, and that setting up trade agencies was to be tightly restricted.

**July 1988**   State Council announced 22 provisions intended to encourage investment by Taiwan businesses.

**Late 1988**   Tightened control on trade and economic links with Taiwan.

**March 1989**   Announced special and preferential treatment to Taiwan investors in the mainland. Themes included permission to develop industrial property and to purchase securities and real estate.

**May 1989**   State Council agreed to set up "Taiwan investment zones" and "Taiwan industrial zones" in Fujian and Hainan.

**July 1989**   Limited the number of companies importing Taiwan products to 68. The number of companies exporting mainland products to Taiwan was not restricted.

**February 1990**   Extended preferential provisions to Taiwan investors. Themes included tax, investment areas, and means.

## Chart 5.1 (continued)
## Recent Policy Changes regarding Cross-Strait Relations

### Taiwan's Policy toward Economic Links with Mainland China

**1979** The Cabinet announced the ban on imports from the mainland except for some herbal medicine and agricultural and industrial raw materials.

**1984** Relaxed restrictions on indirect exports to the mainland through Hong Kong and Macao.

**July 1985** Declared the principles regarding trade with Hong Kong and Macao: no direct trade with the mainland, no contact with mainland official organizations and staff, and no interfering with indirect trade.

**July 1987** Allowed imports of 27 more agricultural and industrial raw materials from the mainland. In November, lifted the ban on visits to the mainland by citizens.

**August 1988** Ministry of Economic Affairs allowed the import of 50 mainland products. Bureau of International Trade implemented a monitor system on indirect exports to the mainland. In December, Bureau of International Trade transferred illegal mainland imports to the jurisdiction of the Customs. Minor violations were no longer punished.

**January 1989** Extended the list of mainland imports to 90 items.

**March 1989** Bureau of International Trade asserted again the ban on participation by Taiwan businesses in commercial exhibitions in the mainland.

**June 1989** Promulgated a statute coping with the handling of mainland products.

**Early 1990** Extended the list of mainland imports to 155 items.

**July 1990** The Ministry of Economic Affairs passed a regulation governing indirect exports to the mainland and another governing investment and technological cooperation with the mainland. A positive list was drawn up of 2,500 products for investment in the mainland.

**October 1990** Promulgated the "regulation governing indirect investment and technological cooperation with the mainland." A positive list was announced of 3,353 products for investment in, and technological cooperation with, the mainland.

**1991** Allowed 9 more mainland agricultural and industrial raw materials for import. Extended the positive list for investment in the mainland to 3,679 items. Mainland Affairs Council and Straits-Exchange Foundation were established.

*Source:* Tzong-Ta Yen, "Investment in and Trade with the Mainland by Taiwan Businessmen," Chung-Hua Institution for Economic Research, for the Council for Economic Planning and Development, Taipei, 1992 (in Chinese).

policy. It toned down previous calls for the liberation of Taiwan and called instead for Taiwan's peaceful reunification with the motherland. Although Taiwan responded with two doctrines—"Three no's–no contact, no negotiation, and no compromise" and "Unification through the three principles of the people"—Taiwan nevertheless later discontinued military aggressiveness and gradually loosened restrictions it had placed on indirect contact.

Between 1979 and 1983, trade between Taiwan and the mainland fluctuated because Taiwan's exports to the mainland were significantly affected by the mainland's unstable policies. In 1982 and 1983, Taiwan's mainland exports contracted because the mainland tightened import restrictions in response to economic overheating and growing trade deficits. The mainland's exports to Taiwan, however, expanded steadily except in 1981, when the Hong Kong dollar was devalued against the U.S. dollar (table 5.1).

*1984–1986.*    The mainland made deliberate efforts to attract investors from Taiwan, noting its low land and labor costs as well as the culture and language it shared with Taiwan. In September 1984, control of trade on the mainland devolved to local governments and business sectors, and the central government loosened restrictions on foreign exchange and imports. As a result, Taiwan's exports across the strait surged 111 percent in 1984 and 132 percent in 1985. In July 1985, when the Taiwan government made it clear that it would neither encourage nor interfere with indirect exports to the mainland—that is, exports through a third entity such as Hong Kong—Taiwan's exports to the mainland increased greatly. But imports from the mainland fell in 1985 because of an official Taiwan announcement that these imports were not yet allowed. In 1986, the Communist government once again tightened imports of consumer goods, causing Taiwan's exports to the mainland to fall.

*1987–1994.*    From 1984 to 1986, Taiwan's overall trade surplus reached its peak, causing the N.T. dollar to appreciate enormously. Pressured by a hike in domestic wages and land prices and encouraged by the government's drive for economic liberalization, leaders of Taiwan's export-oriented, labor-intensive industries began to explore investment opportunities abroad, although large-scale outward investment took place only after 1986. Until the end of the 1980s, Taiwan's manufacturing investments were small-scale experiments in the countries of Southeast Asia. As was shown in table 4.3, only after 1989 did Taiwan's investment in the mainland surge and dominate Taiwan's regional investment.

Cross-strait trade has taken an unprecedented turn for the better since 1987, when Taiwan officially allowed imports of 27 more agricultural and industrial raw materials from the mainland and lifted the ban on visits to the mainland by Taiwan citizens. The list of permitted mainland imports continued to lengthen while, at the same time, the Communist government repeatedly publicized its preferential terms to Taiwan investors, thereby attracting investors from Taiwan with great success. Since 1987, two-way trade and investment have expanded steadily and quickly in response to timely policy adjustments by each side.

## Cross-Strait Trade

Cross-strait trade has always responded immediately to changes in the economic policies of each side as well as to factors affecting the bilateral relationship. Recently, the swings have moderated because economic issues have overtaken old political perceptions, and the trend of economic integration across the strait has become increasingly obvious. Still, Taiwan's exports to the mainland have grown more consistently in recent years than mainland exports to Taiwan. This reflects Taipei's steady expansion of investment on the mainland as well as Taiwan's more mature economy.

Trade across the Taiwan Strait has been conducted mainly through Hong Kong (table 5.1), with a smaller part passing through Macao, Okinawa, and other nearby ports.[15] From 1979 to 1993, according to Hong Kong customs statistics, cross-strait trade through Hong Kong increased from $77.8 million to $8.69 billion; Taiwan's exports to the mainland grew from $21.5 million to $7.59 billion, and the mainland's exports to Taiwan expanded from $56.3 million to $1.10 billion. Adjusted statistics compiled by Taiwan's Mainland Affairs Council show much higher yet more realistic estimates of cross-strait trade: the figure of $0.5 billion in 1981 rose to $15.1 billion in 1993. Mainland Affairs Council figures, however, are consistent with Hong Kong customs statistics on Taiwan's trade dependence on the mainland, which remained steady between 1981 and 1986 but grew to 9.3 percent in 1993.

Trade dependence, or bilateral trade as a percentage of total trade, climbed between 1979 and 1993: it rose from 0.3 percent to 9.3 percent for Taiwan vis-à-vis the mainland and from 0.3 percent to 7.7 percent for the mainland vis-à-vis Taiwan (table 5.2). Taiwan's export dependence on the mainland, measured by its exports to the mainland as a percentage of Taiwan's total exports, increased from 0.1 percent to 16.5 percent between 1979 and 1993; export dependence of the mainland on Taiwan increased from 0.4 percent to 1.2 percent during the same period. Taiwan's dependence on the mainland for imports rose from 0.4 percent to 1.4 percent, and the mainland's dependence on Taiwan rose from 0.1 percent to 13.5 percent.

***Commodity Composition.*** Significant changes have occurred in the commodity composition of Taiwan-mainland trade. In 1979, textile yarn and fabrics accounted for 81.4 percent of Taiwan's total exports to the mainland; plastic materials, machinery, electrical parts, and other goods constituted the rest. But by 1993, the textiles share had fallen to 30.2 percent, although it remained the largest category of Taiwan's exports to the mainland. Other products such as machinery, electronics and electrical parts, and plastic materials increased in importance; in 1993, these products together accounted for 37.1 percent, and other products made up the remaining 32.7 percent.

Chinese medicine and other animal and vegetable materials have been the largest category of Taiwan imports from the mainland, but their share shrank from 82.5 percent in 1979 to 10.5 percent in 1993. Increased trade in semifinished products, textiles, and electrical goods indicates that, over time, Taiwan has experienced a trade creation effect as a result of its cross-strait trade (see charts 5.2 and 5.3).

Initially, cross-strait trade depended on a limited number of products. More recently, a greater variety of goods has been traded. Products in the same category have begun to appear on lists of both exports and imports, implying an extension from vertical interindustry trade to horizontal intraindustry trade.[16]

***Interdependence.*** In 1994, Taiwan and the mainland each became the other's fourth largest trading partner. Taiwan has been alert to its growing economic dependence on the mainland because the mainland's policy on economic links with Taiwan has been extremely politicized.

**Chart 5.2**
**Top 20 Export Items from Mainland China to Taiwan,**
**January 1994–July 1994**
(in millions of U.S. dollars)

| Rank | SITC Code | Description | $ Amount | % Share |
|------|-----------|-------------|----------|---------|
| 1 | 292.4 | Herbal medicine | 42.1 | 6.01 |
| 2 | 85190 | Semi-finished shoes and boots | 33.0 | 4.71 |
| 3 | 65331 | Woven mixed-fiber fabrics of primarily cotton content | 30.6 | 4.37 |
| 4 | 29195 | Birds' feathers | 28.7 | 4.10 |
| 5 | 77119 | Misc. electric substation equipment | 24.6 | 3.51 |
| 6 | 88114 | Photographic equipment and flash accessories | 12.4 | 1.77 |
| 7 | 77125 | Misc. induction machines | 11.8 | 1.68 |
| 8 | 68611 | Zinc (non-gold) | 10.6 | 1.52 |
| 9 | 76493 | Accessories, components for threadless rotating instruments | 10.3 | 1.47 |
| 10 | 03411 | Raw, fresh, and live fish products (principally eel fry) | 9.4 | 1.34 |
| 11 | 65221 | Unbleached knit fabric of over 85 percent cotton content weighing under 200 grams | 9.2 | 1.31 |
| 12 | 77121 | Motionless electric system equipment | 8.1 | 1.16 |
| 13 | 65133 | Cotton yarn | 8.1 | 1.16 |
| 14 | 77631 | Diodes | 7.9 | 1.13 |
| 15 | 84530 | Pullover collarless, open-neck shirts and vests | 7.9 | 1.13 |
| 16 | 71610 | Electric-powered rotating machinery not exceeding 37.5 watts | 7.8 | 1.11 |
| 17 | 75997 | Automatic handling equipment and components | 7.3 | 1.04 |
| 18 | 77812 | Battery storage cells | 6.3 | 0.90 |
| 19 | 82159 | Misc. wooden furniture | 6.0 | 0.86 |
| 20 | 65360 | Recycled woven cotton fiber of over 85 percent recycled cotton fiber content | 5.9 | 0.84 |
| **Total** | | | **288.0** | **41.10** |

*Sources:* Mainland Affairs Council, Taipei, *Monthly Statistics of Cross-Strait Economic Activities,* various issues.

**Table 5.3**
**Top 20 Export Items from Taiwan to Mainland China,**
**January 1994–July 1994**
(in millions of U.S. dollars)

| Rank | SITC code | Description | $ Amount | % Share |
|------|-----------|-------------|----------|---------|
| 1 | 65732 | Fiber derivative and other man-made plastic dying cloth materials | 259.9 | 5.54 |
| 2 | 65314 | Synthetic woven fabric | 202.8 | 4.32 |
| 3 | 65529 | Misc. knitted or hooked fabrics | 169.0 | 3.60 |
| 4 | 58224 | PVC plates, sheets, etc. | 147.2 | 3.14 |
| 5 | 65152 | Polyester fabrics, not for retail sale | 146.4 | 3.12 |
| 6 | 57292 | Alkene and benzene polymers | 143.5 | 3.06 |
| 7 | 78513 | Bicycles equipped with added power | 104.7 | 2.23 |
| 8 | 76493 | Accessories and components for threadless rotating instruments | 103.3 | 2.20 |
| 9 | 65315 | Semiprocessed curtain fabric of synthetic fibers | 101.8 | 2.17 |
| 10 | 61141 | Horse and cow leather goods | 77.4 | 1.65 |
| 11 | 68241 | Refined copper wire | 75.0 | 1.60 |
| 12 | 65523 | Misc. knit goods (including machine knit) | 71.8 | 1.53 |
| 13 | 77129 | Unassembled electrical and mechanical components | 59.3 | 1.26 |
| 14 | 57219 | Misc. unprocessed combination of benzene and alkene | 58.8 | 1.25 |
| 15 | 72842 | Unassembled mechanical appliances of man-made latex | 54.4 | 1.16 |
| 16 | 65316 | Misc. machine-woven goods containing over 85 percent unprocessed esters silk | 50.4 | 1.07 |
| 17 | 75997 | Automatic machines and attachments | 50.2 | 1.07 |
| 18 | 58229 | Misc. plastic boards and strips | 47.6 | 1.01 |
| 19 | 89949 | Umbrellas and sunshades — components and attachments | 47.1 | 1.00 |
| 20 | 65184 | Yarn of less than 85 percent synthetic fiber content, not for retail use | 44.7 | 0.95 |
| **Total** | | | **2,015.3** | **42.94** |

*Source:*   Mainland Affairs Council, Taipei, *Monthly Statistics of Cross-Strait Economic Activities*, various issues.

Taiwan's dependence on trade with the mainland exceeds the converse. Taiwan's land area is only 0.4 percent that of the mainland; its GNP is approximately 40 percent as large as the mainland's; and it is about 2.4 times more dependent on external trade than the mainland. These facts raise the question of whether Taiwan is more vulnerable than the mainland to disruption of cross-strait economic activities.

Taiwan's increasing economic dependence on the mainland is not merely an economic but also a political issue. Because the mainland has blocked or hampered Taiwan's participation in international organizations and because Taiwan has never been completely able to rule out a military threat from the mainland, many in Taiwan are uneasy regarding Taiwan's growing dependence on trade with the mainland. This disquiet contrasts with passiveness over Taiwan's high dependence on trade with the United States and Japan.

*Trade Balance.* Several reasons underlie Taiwan's increasing trade surplus with the mainland. Since 1980, Taiwan has exported to the mainland higher-value-added products such as sophisticated raw materials, machinery, equipment, and electronic parts while imports from the mainland have been relatively low-value-added products such as crude raw materials, consumer nondurables, and food products. The unit value of Taiwan's exports to the mainland, by any measure, tends to be higher than its imports from the mainland.

Second, the Communist government has blamed Taiwan for the imbalance, citing Taiwan's restrictions on imports from the mainland. But, according to Hong Kong customs data, most of the top 20 mainland exports to Taiwan are not on Taiwan's official list of permitted items, implying that Taiwan's governmental estrictions on indirect trade are of little consequence.[17]

The cross-strait trade imbalance is largely a structural issue: a bilateral trade imbalance may not be a problem so long as Taiwan's total external trade is balanced and the bilateral trade imbalance is the result of market forces and not official constraints.

## Competition between Beijing and Taipei in Major Markets

Two of the major markets in which Taiwan and the mainland compete for market share are the United States and Japan.

*In the United States.*    In 1992, the United States imported from Taiwan $24.5 billion worth of products, accounting for 4.7 percent of U.S. total imports, and imported from the mainland $25.5 billion, accounting for 4.9 percent. Since 1988, U.S. imports from Taiwan have expanded more slowly than before, with years when there was no increase and any rate of increase falling from double to single digits. In contrast, U.S. imports from the mainland have expanded between 20 percent and 40 percent each year since 1983 (table 5.3). As a result, the relative size of Taiwan's exports to the United States shrank from being almost five times as great as mainland exports in 1983 to only 96 percent of the mainland's exports in 1993. The mainland has become Taiwan's chief competitor for U.S. market share even though Taiwan's businessmen have played an increasingly important role in the mainland's exports to the United States.

As far as major export products are concerned, there is little direct competition between Taiwan and the mainland. Technology-intensive products such as information system components and electronics are Taiwan's major export items to the United States; the mainland claims a very small share of the U.S. market for these products. On the other hand, Taiwan's former staple export items—toys, footwear, textiles, and apparel—evidence a declining share and have now become the mainland's major exports to the United States.

Among each economy's top 30 export items to the United States, plastic products, stuffed toys, and small parts for automatic data processing machines are common to both. Taiwan has already lost to the mainland its U.S. market for toys, except for stuffed toys, and the prospects for plastic products and even stuffed toys do not seem promising to Taiwan. Both sides' shares in the U.S. market are increasing for parts used in automatic data processing machines although the mainland's share is increasing faster. Many of Taiwan's traditional export items to the U.S. market are expected to continue to lose their competitive edge to the mainland.

*In Japan.*    In 1992, Japan imported $9.4 billion worth of Taiwan products, or 4.1 percent of Japan's total imports; Japan imported $16.9 billion worth of mainland products, equivalent to 7.3 percent. Exports to Japan from both Taiwan and the mainland have grown, with Taiwan's share about half the mainland's (table 5.4).

The composition of Taiwan's exports to Japan is again quite different from the mainland's. Among Taiwan's major exports to Japan are live animals, fishery products, other animal products, and electronic information products. The mainland's major items are textiles, crude petroleum, agricultural products, toys, footwear, and other industrial raw materials and products requiring only low-skilled labor to manufacture.

The average skill level required to produce Taiwan's exports to Japan is higher than that required for mainland exports. Taiwan's share of skill-intensive products is larger than the mainland's, demonstrating Taiwan's relative advantage in these products. The bulk of the mainland's exports to Japan are labor-intensive and low-skill products such as garments and footwear. These had been Taiwan's primary exports to Japan but have decreased because Taiwan's comparative advantage has shifted.

Some of the increase in mainland exports to the United States and Japan stems from foreign ventures in the mainland. Foreign investors, mainly from Hong Kong, Taiwan, Japan, and the United States, have been attracted to mainland China because of its relatively inexpensive labor. Because its shifting comparative advantage causes labor-intensive industries to fade, Taiwan needs to develop high-technology and high-end products to maintain its position in world trade.

## Taiwan's Investment in the Mainland

As part of its macroeconomic adjustments, Taiwan's overseas investment has increased rapidly since the late 1980s. Since the November 1987 lifting of the ban on visits from Taiwan to the mainland, Taiwan investment in the mainland has increased significantly. On a contracted basis, Taiwan businessmen are second only to their Hong Kong neighbors in establishing investment projects in the mainland and are far ahead of the Japanese, who were the third largest investors in the mainland in 1992 (tables 5.5 and 5.6).

In 1993, Taiwan's contracted investment in the mainland covered 10,948 projects and was estimated to be $9.97 billion. Investment per project averaged less than $1 million, much smaller than other foreign investments in the mainland. The modest size of each project results in part from a Taiwan regulation that requires any investment on the mainland exceeding $1 million to go through a company in a third country. Also, larger investments require more study and planning. The number of investments is on the rise, however, and, as operational scope expands, more economies of scale are expected to materialize.

In the beginning, most Taiwan investors formed joint ventures with local mainland businesses. To gain more autonomy and reduce management inefficiency, they now prefer to set up wholly owned plants. Investors also tend now to be corporations rather than individuals. Both these changes are not uncommon developments.

In general, Taiwan investments have been short-term, small-scale, quick to set up, and quick to turn a profit. Recently, however, there have been signs of long-term planning. New investments tend to be larger. Plant sites and buildings are no longer rented but are self-owned or self-built. One common feature remains: most of these investments still need Taiwan's distribution system.

***Sectoral Composition.*** According to the Republic of China Investment Commission, the top five industries favored by Taiwan businesses between 1991 and 1993 were electronics and electrical appliances, with a cumulative investment of $511 million or 14.2 percent of Taiwan's total investment in the mainland; plastic products, with investment of $439 million or 12.2 percent; food and beverages, with $389 million invested or 10.8 percent; precision instruments, amounting to $311 million or 8.7 percent; and products made of base metals, totaling $274 million or 7.6 percent (table 5.7). In general, most investments were made in labor-intensive processing industries.

***Geographical Distribution.*** The five areas that hosted the bulk of Taiwan investment between 1991 and 1993 were Guangdong Province, with investment totaling $462 million or 12.9 percent of Taiwan's total investment in the mainland; Shanghai, where investment totaled $449 million or 12.5 percent; Jiangsu Province, $444 million or 12.4 percent; Shenzhen Special Economic Zone, $315 million or 8.8 percent; and Dongguan (in Guangdong Province), $263 million or 7.3 percent (table 5.8). Fujian is nearest to Taiwan and was significant until around 1990, but other coastal areas have gained in importance more recently. Since 1992, mainland China has gradually opened its local markets to foreign ventures and has extended economic openness to more industries and geographical areas, thus attracting some Taiwanese investments to cities in the interior.

*Operations.* Initially, most of Taiwan's manufacturing investments in the mainland originated from industries attempting to retain market share as their competitive edge in Taiwan eroded. Investors from these industries took machinery, raw materials, and intermediate inputs, mainly from Taiwan but also from other countries, to produce in the mainland. They later sold their products overseas through their existing trade networks. This has helped build a high export ratio for Taiwan enterprises in the mainland but has also contributed to the decrease of traditional Taiwan exports of footwear, umbrellas, toys, garments, and bicycles to developed country markets. Although its current trade advantage rests on more capital- and technology-intensive products, Taiwan continues to develop new export products to maintain its export strength.

Mainland purchases of raw materials, equipment, and components from Taiwan have contributed to the rapid increase in Taiwan's cross-strait exports. Over time, Taiwan firms will increase their purchases of raw materials and semifinished products from mainland suppliers as mainland industries become capable of providing these goods. This trend is analogous to the shift to local sourcing by multinational corporations in Taiwan.[18] As foreign investments help create local demand for intermediate goods and upgrade relevant local industries, foreign supplies are substituted by goods produced by the host economy; this process is known as backward linkage.

According to a government survey, more than 60 percent of Taiwan-funded factories in the mainland depend on production technologies originating in their parent companies, and over half import materials and machinery from Taiwan.[19] Of these investors, 31 percent reported profits, and another 26 percent reported a balanced financial status or small profit margins. Those who claimed losses accounted for 39.1 percent.

*Reexports to Taiwan.* Taiwan manufacturers in the mainland have an export ratio of about 85 percent, much higher than the average export ratio (below 30 percent for other foreign ventures, which aim at domestic sales). The reason is straightforward: most Taiwan enterprises in the mainland are export-oriented because the mainland government restricts local sales. In the past year or two, however, the mainland government has moved toward removing curbs on domestic sales; when curbs are removed, the export ratio of Taiwan-invested firms should decrease.

Products manufactured by Taiwan-invested firms are exported mainly to Hong Kong, the United States, Japan, and Europe. More than 95 percent of miscellaneous industrial production is exported, with over 80 percent shipped to the United States and Japan. The export ratio for transportation equipment, mainly bicycles, also exceeds 80 percent, with the major markets being in the United States and Europe. Hong Kong is the most important market for electric and electronic products, garments, and other manufactured goods, while Japan is the principal market for wood and bamboo products.

Some products are shipped back to Taiwan. According to a survey by the Chung-Hua Institution for Economic Research in Taiwan, about 25 percent of Taiwan firms in the mainland ship products back home. But the government survey mentioned above shows that only 5.8 percent of goods made in the mainland are sold back to Taiwan, and 50 percent of these are semifinished products for further processing.

Industries with higher reexport-to-Taiwan ratios are precision machinery, machine equipment, chemicals, pulp and paper, plastics, wood, and base metals. Those with lower ratios are food, beverages, fur and leather, metals, transportation equipment, and garments. According to the Chung-Hua Institution for Economic Research, the average reexport ratio of this second group is about 12 percent.

## Scenarios for the Future

*Hong Kong.*   Hong Kong plays a key role in Taiwan-mainland interchange. Although indirect cross-strait exchanges are permitted, travel, investment, trade, and financial flows all must be conducted through a third party. As the gateway to and from the mainland, Hong Kong has been the most important intermediary between interested parties in Taiwan and the mainland.

Hong Kong's share of Taiwan's foreign trade increased from 5.5 percent in 1987 to 12.5 percent in 1993. In 1993, Hong Kong was Taiwan's third largest trading partner, with bilateral trade reaching $20.2 billion. Also in 1993, Taiwan exported $18.4 billion worth of goods to Hong Kong, which since 1990 has been Taiwan's second most important export market. Taiwan imported $1.7 billion of goods from Hong Kong in 1993. The bilateral balance was $16.7 billion in Taiwan's favor, double Taiwan's total trade surplus. In other words, without its surplus with Hong Kong, Taiwan would run trade deficits. The Republic of China Board of Foreign Trade estimates that the surplus with Hong Kong was $21.3 billion in 1994, making it Taiwan's largest bilateral surplus for the fourth consecutive year.

When the mainland began economic reforms in 1979, indirect exports from Taiwan to the mainland accounted for only 1.9 percent of Taiwan's total exports to Hong Kong. Hong Kong's importance as an entrepôt in cross-strait trade increased as that figure surged to 20 percent in 1981 and to 39 percent in 1985. By 1993, it registered 76 percent. Between January and June 1994, Hong Kong imported $9.9 billion, or 23 percent, of Taiwan's total export value. Customs statistics indicate that products worth about $6.7 billion, or 67 percent, that were exported to Hong Kong were forwarded to mainland China.

In 1979, indirect imports from the mainland accounted for 27.5 percent of Taiwan's total imports from Hong Kong; this ratio remained steady between 30 percent and 40 percent in the decade that followed. In 1991, this figure approached 60 percent. The upward trend probably reflects the effect of Taiwan's continuing removal of restrictions on the import of mainland products.

According to mainland sources, through the end of 1993 Taiwan investors in the mainland signed more than 18,000 investment contracts worth about $19 billion. The great majority of the ventures were set up through some 3,000 branch offices in Hong Kong. Because, as noted earlier, Taiwan law requires that investment projects in the mainland of more than $1 million be made through a company in a third country, Hong Kong has been the most convenient middleman for indirect investment flows.

Considerable financial flows are needed to facilitate cross-strait investment and trade. Because of its well-developed international financial infrastructure, Hong Kong has been the preferred financial intermediary for Taiwan investors and traders. Even after 1991, when the Taiwan government first permitted foreign exchange operations in Taiwan to facilitate the exports of Taiwan firms operating in the mainland, Hong Kong has remained the top choice for Taiwan traders. Hong Kong is popular because of its convenience and efficiency, tax incentives, flexible financial channels, and freedom from Taiwan's regulations. Because of the absence in the mainland of an adequate financial infrastructure, Taiwan-funded firms there also rely on the Hong Kong market to acquire foreign exchange.

The complementarity among Taiwan, Hong Kong, and mainland China has encouraged their economic integration and has reinforced the comparative advantages of each economy. The mainland is endowed with abundant land, labor, and natural resources and has an adequate technological foundation. Taiwan offers capital, extensive trade experience, many applied technologies, and managerial skills. Hong Kong is blessed with world-class financial network and port facilities, efficient market distribution systems, and highly capable management. The economic logic that draws Taiwan to the mainland through Hong Kong is therefore apparent; it has been so powerful that indirect Taiwan-mainland economic ties have developed very rapidly and intensively, increasing the importance of Hong Kong's intermediary position.

Despite the recent rift between London and Beijing over Hong Kong's democratic reforms, the fact is that on July 1, 1997, the mainland will assume sovereignty over Hong Kong and rule it as a Special Administration Region.

The impact of Hong Kong's return to mainland China's rule remains to be seen. In the long run, because Hong Kong is a showcase to China's people of a modern society with a workable judicial framework, Hong Kong's return will help pressure the mainland government to change. Yet Hong Kong's future will be shaped by the mainland's domestic politics and foreign policy.

One possible development, if no significant detour occurs in the mainland's current general policies, is that Hong Kong's existing system and advantages will be preserved and its respectable growth continue.

Alternatively, if no great change of direction occurs in the mainland's reform but the pace of development decelerates because of more inhibiting measures and controls, Hong Kong could become more socialistic, a development that would deter foreign investment. Hong Kong's free market spirit could be weakened and its prestigious position as a financial and transportation center in Southeast Asia could suffer.

If the leadership in the mainland is dominated by more ambitious reformers, the momentum of reform will increase and the economy will be further opened and liberalized. Most likely, Hong Kong would be given a free hand to develop its capitalist system, and democrats there would be able to continue political reform. In this case, the scope of economic integration among Hong Kong, Taiwan, and the mainland will expand and fill out. Hong Kong may also have to compete with other major cities in the mainland—Shanghai, for instance—as a gateway to the mainland.

If the hard-liners take the reins, however, reversals may occur in the mainland's economic reform policy. Although the mainland is unlikely to close completely again, instability and uncertainty will grow. This development will frighten investors, and Hong Kong's attractiveness will decline. If Hong Kong is repressed, other cities in the East Asian region will rise to take its place among the Asian financial capitals.

**Security and Economics.** In July 1992, the Taipei Airline Business Association wrote to Taiwan's Ministry of Transportation and Communications proposing the establishment of direct cross-strait transport. The association argued that direct flights could increase business profits and reduce costs. Currently, Taiwan's airlines enjoy 21 percent of the market on the Taiwan-Hong Kong-mainland route. If a direct connection were allowed, the member firms of the association estimate they could increase their share to 50 percent. Even with a fall in ticket prices, they expect their profits to rise by more than $30 million. Passengers from Taiwan could save up to $4 million in the aggregate.[20]

Besides air links, direct sea links are also being proposed. Currently, cross-strait marine lines must go through Hong Kong or Okinawa. Direct lines would not only reduce costs and shipping time, but also eliminate many shipping documents.

Because costs vary considerably with the type of cargo, actual cost savings have yet to be determined. Various factors must be considered: first, if the volume of cargo occupies less than 60 percent of the capacity of any given vessel, direct marine transport is not profitable; second, because ports in the mainland are in poor condition and facilities are inadequate, foreign vessels must pay extra fees to expedite service; third, there are large differences in the volumes of the two-way cargo flows. Although the flow from Taiwan to the mainland is heavy, it takes three to six months to fill a container in the mainland for the return trip to Taiwan. Some studies therefore predict that even with direct shipping lines, some freighters may still prefer indirect lines to handle cross-strait marine cargo.

Arguments against direct cross-strait transportation originate with the concept of national identity and economic impact. Because the mainland recognizes neither Taiwan's sovereignty nor the nationality of Taiwan's aircraft and vessels, entrance and exit documentation would be a paramount problem requiring resolution before any direct transport links could be opened. Nationality also poses problems for other related activities such as navigation, communications, quarantine inspection, taxation, and dispute settlement.

After direct transport links, both sealines and airlines, are opened, direct business transactions will follow, with faster capital flows to the mainland and a much more convenient transportation environment developed because the volume of goods shipped by Taiwan's upgraded industries, both in and out of the mainland, will continue to boom. Taiwan, however, may have an additional benefit by turning itself into a regional transportation hub.

*Integration.*   Further economic integration of the mainland and Taiwan is contingent on the expansion of industrial interdependence and the development of political dialogue. Further industrial integration hinges on the transformation of the political platform on both sides of the Taiwan Strait. This does not mean that political stagnancy will necessarily undermine economic interests. Nonetheless, political and economic developments are interdependent. The outlook will be bright if the increased economic welfare growing out of mutual contacts softens political rigidity and if economic integration advances to further demonstrate the advantages of combining the economies of Taiwan, Hong Kong, and the mainland in all possible ways.

Details must be negotiated if economic cooperation is to take fuller shape. But because the mainland still does not recognize Taiwan as a political entity, direct negotiations are confined to modest, low-level talks. The development of industrial and technical cooperation could be hampered by lack of official recognition.

Nevertheless, Taiwan is working diligently to bypass the political arena to forge further economic integration. To this end, a large conference on the development of cross-strait commercial relations was held in July 1994 at which the following tasks were sketched out:

- Study the cross-strait division of labor and industrial specialization and devise supporting industrial policies to promote economic synergy.

- Explore ways and means to protect Taiwan business interests in the mainland. These include negotiating an investment protection agreement with the mainland, encouraging Taiwan businesses to form associations to assist one another, helping new investors to establish themselves, and setting up dispute resolution channels and provisions.

- Review and promote agricultural and fishery exchanges, including the exchange of information, technology, breeds, and other resources. The prevention and settlement of disputes between fishermen from the two sides are also central to the Taiwan government's goals.

- Develop more channels and means for two-way financial flows, create more opportunities for Taiwan banks, and keep more accurate data on capital movements.

- Open indirect insurance business exchanges. The Ministry of Finance and the Mainland Affairs Council will work together to promote such exchanges and draw up plans to help Taiwan insurers set up outlets in the mainland.

- Establish, under the International Monetary Fund framework, a balance-of-payments account among Taiwan, Hong Kong, and the mainland to provide policymakers with a reliable reference regarding triangular monetary interchanges.

- Cooperate with the mainland to curb smuggling.

- Study the feasibility of direct transport links.

*WTO Membership.* Both Taiwan and the mainland are actively seeking membership in the WTO. Taiwan is now an observer of that world trade body and has entered into the final stages of trade negotiations with its contracting members. Very soon, representatives from both sides of the strait will have to meet under multilateral auspices. Each party will need to decide how to deal with the other on economic issues before entering any serious negotiations.

When Taiwan and the mainland join the WTO, Taiwan will feel threatened by the mainland's export of agricultural products to Taiwan. Because of their geographic advantage and significant differences in production costs, mainland farmers will certainly outproduce their Taiwan counterparts. Taiwan's farmers are already under mounting pressure from increasing imports from the United States, Australia, and New Zealand. Imports from the mainland upon WTO membership could be a further shock to Taiwan's agricultural sector.

In nonagricultural areas, the mainland will have to lower tariffs and remove import controls after joining the WTO, expanding the export market for Taiwan. The opening of tertiary industries and infrastructural construction will offer Taiwan businesses greater investment opportunities, possibly exacerbating capital exodus and industrial relocation from Taiwan and enhancing cross-strait economic interaction. Issues that remain to be resolved are related not to the direction of economic integration but to its optimal pace.

# 6

# Taiwan as a Regional Operations Center

*As a solution*

Two major trends have recently emerged: the globalization of corporate business and regional economic integration. In globalizing their activities, corporate planners know well the Asia-Pacific's importance as the world's most dynamic market and a major center of production. Alert companies are spreading their operations around the region, and, as regional economic growth gains momentum, these companies will have to set up regional operations centers to manage decision-making about not only production but also distribution, financing, research and development (R&D), and all other regional business activities.

The idea underlying a regional operations center is the assignment of decision-making authority by a parent company to a local division or subsidiary responsible for all regional production, distribution, and R&D. Through such decentralization, local information is used more efficiently, particularly where coordination problems exist between or among regions. Devolution of decision-making authority to the regional level promotes geographical specialization and division of labor. It also stimulates regional coordination, such as the building of transportation networks.

A step beyond a regional operations center is the concept of a regional profits center or multiple profits center. By establishing profits centers in different parts of the world—in Europe, in Asia and the Pacific, and in North America—a parent company would be less vulnerable to developments in the economy in which it is based. Rather, it can diversify risk by holding shares of its profits center corporations in other countries. A parent company can also benefit by listing its financially independent, profit-earning subsidiary on the local stock market or simply by raising funds in the local market.

Regional operations centers become desirable when intraregional trade is growing and when significant institutional and behavioral differences exist between markets in the East and

West. Because intraregional trade is increasing in Asia and rapidly changing market conditions call for fast responses, establishing a regional operations center may be more cost-effective than setting up numerous corporate divisions within the region that report individually to the parent company.

## Taiwan and Regional Operations

Because of its central position in the Asia-Pacific region, its close links with the West, and the strength of its local economy, Taiwan has emerged as an attractive site for companies contemplating the establishment of an Asia-Pacific regional operations center.

Taiwan's economic transition since the 1980s, rooted in the sharp appreciation of the NT dollar and in efforts to adjust to macroeconomic imbalances, has resulted in an extraordinarily high trade surplus and declining investment growth. Taiwan's industrialists were quick to translate their new comparative advantage into a survival strategy in a world of intensifying competition. They invested their appreciated local currency in neighboring economies and improved the efficiency of local production. Although unaware of their impact on Taiwan's future economy, these entrepreneurs were equipping Taiwan with the capability and skills to perform regional operations.

These capabilities were based on Taiwan's intraregional economic ties and position, international trade network, resilient domestic economy, and domestic stability.

*Intraregional Economic Ties and Position.*    Taiwan is well situated geographically for coordinating trade among China, Southeast Asia, Japan, and North America. Culturally, Taiwan is a Chinese society with much in common with Singapore, Hong Kong, mainland China, and the enormous overseas Chinese communities throughout Southeast Asia. Taiwan also shares a Confucian tradition with non-Chinese societies in Japan and the Republic of Korea (South Korea).

Although current regulations governing cross-strait activities have put some restraints on Taiwan businesses, many Taiwan firms have, in effect, set up production branches in the mainland by receiving the export orders in Taiwan and then delivering the orders from the mainland to a third country. Taiwan's industrial structure and its science and technology base are solid, especially in the areas of manufacturing, technical manpower, and R&D.

Taiwan's extensive intraregional ties include trade, investment, and technological exchange. Taiwan's trade with Asia amounted to $69.2 billion for the first 11 months of 1993, with Japan and Hong Kong taking the lion's share. Indirect trade with mainland China has grown very fast: trade across the Taiwan Strait through Hong Kong increased 30-fold, from $0.2 billion to $7.4 billion, in the decade beginning in 1983.

Trade with ASEAN members has also expanded remarkably: between 1986 and 1992, ASEAN's share of Taiwan's total exports rose from less than 5 percent to 10 percent, while its share of Taiwan's total imports increased from 6 percent to 8 percent.

In addition, almost one-third of Taiwan's outward investment is directed to ASEAN. Taiwan's cumulative investment in ASEAN and Vietnam surpassed $16 billion in 1993 (see table 4.5).

***International Trade Network.*** Although its assumption of a pivotal role in the Asia-Pacific region is recent, Taiwan has a long history of close ties with Western countries, with Japan, and, increasingly, with the European countries.

These trade and investment flows have made Taiwan's economy export-led since the beginning of its modern development. In 1993, Taiwan's two-way trade amounted to $157.2 billion,[21] making it the world's thirteenth largest trader. Since the 1960s,Taiwan has been closely integrated with Northeast Asia, including Japan and South Korea. More recently, Taiwan's ambitious overseas investment has expanded Taiwan's trade web into Southeast Asia and the mainland. In 1994, about 35 percent of Taiwan's total trade was with South Korea, Japan, Hong Kong, and the mainland, a substantial increase from 25 percent in 1989. Taiwan has also been an attractive site in the Asia-Pacific region for overseas investment from Western countries.

Taiwan's capital inflows and outflows helped build its substantial trade network, which is the mainstay for effective regional marketing and international business management. And it is from the trade network base that additional trade, financial activities, and other businesses can be developed.

***Resilient Domestic Economy and Domestic Stability.***[22] In 1993, Taiwan's GNP reached $220 billion, the twentieth highest in the world. In the same year, per capita GNP was $10,600, the twenty-fifth highest among countries with a population of more than 1 million. Despite its recent slowdown, common among maturing economies, Taiwan's economy grew 5.9 percent in 1993 and 6.5 percent in 1994 and is targeted to grow a little faster—6.8 percent—in 1995.

With per capita income around $11,000, Taiwan's population of 21 million represents a consumer market with enormous purchasing power. Private consumption has been expanding by double-digit rates since 1987, the year after the NT dollar began its rapid appreciation and the domestic market quickened. In 1994, nominal private consumption growth was targeted for 11 percent. Both the ongoing six-year infrastructural plan, which was scaled down somewhat in 1994, and the promotion program for private investment provide great opportunities for foreign capital, goods, and services.

## Challenges and Limitations

For all its advantages, Taiwan also has its drawbacks. Infrastructure, such as transportation and communications, needs augmentation; land prices are increasing; and laws and regulations need to be updated to facilitate rather than hamper trade, investment, and financial activities.

Infrastructural investment has played an important role in Taiwan's rapid economic development. In the 1970s, increasing public investment helped break through the decade's development bottleneck. In the early 1980s, public investment was cut back to foster private sector development. However, both public and private investment weakened, resulting in insufficient public investment in both hardware and software. This affected domestic and international transportation, telecommunications, and power supply, all important in building a supportive infrastructure for regional or global operations.

Prices of non-tradable goods have escalated considerably since the late 1980s due to mounting trade surpluses and excessive expansion of the money supply. In addition to real estate and stocks, industrial land has become extremely expensive. Taiwan's land prices are much higher than prices in the ASEAN-4 countries and, in fact, are comparable with those in Hong Kong, Singapore, and South Korea.

Taiwan began liberalizing its trade and foreign exchange regulations in the 1960s. But even in the early 1980s, a relatively high level of tariffs and trade barriers were still in place. Liberalization accelerated as the economy matured and pressure mounted from all directions. Taiwan's prospective entry into the GATT has reinforced this liberalization; targets for opening are the only details remaining.

In addition to liberalization, reform of existing regulations in many areas is also important for providing good institutional infrastructure for international operations. Reforms will facilitate immigration and customs procedures; revise aviation, marine, and telecommunications regulations; update accounting and financial laws; and nurture international law specialists. The government has committed itself to construct in Taiwan a friendly environment for globalization.

## Infrastructural Development

In 1991, the Taiwan government launched the six-year National Development Plan to provide the country with the infrastructural software and hardware needed to increase overall productivity and improve the national quality of life. This comprehensive plan proposes a series of public construction projects to strengthen infrastructural development, boost industrial growth, and balance development between the counties and cities. These projects will dramatically improve transportation and communications, public utilities, urban construction and housing, manufacturing industries, environmental protection, and medical care.

*Telecommunications.* Taiwan's plans for a comprehensive telecommunications network for domestic and international information exchange call for the acceleration of network digitalization and promotion of optical fiber transmission.

*Transportation.* The new transport network should provide safe and high-speed inland transportation with efficient connections to international maritime and air transportation. Projects include a high-speed railway along Taiwan's western corridor, a second north-south freeway, other island-wide highway networks, and mass rapid transit systems for major cities.

A marine and aviation transport program includes the expansion of container facilities at Kaohsiung harbor and the modernization of domestic and international airports, thereby improving harbor and airport administration, flight control, and customs.

In early 1994, Taiwan's minister of economic affairs proposed the idea of direct city-to-city or harbor-to-harbor shipments to the mainland rather than indirect shipments through Hong Kong. If acted on this suggestion will enhance Taiwan's competitiveness by greatly reducing the cost of cross-strait transportation.

*Service Industries.* High-quality services will be required to meet the wide range of demands from regional business operations. Taiwan's six-year development plan includes updating laws and regulations, manpower planning, and spatial programming of services distribution. Service sector output is targeted to grow 7.8 percent and employment should grow 3.4 percent during 1991 through 1996. The growth target for insurance services is 14.8 percent, and for financial services, excluding insurance, 9.1 percent.

## Institutional Reform—Deregulation and Reregulation

Taiwan's economic policy has been moving toward liberalization and internationalization. Its trade and financial liberalization give evidence of the outward-looking strategy Taiwan has pursued since it began its rapid development at the beginning of the 1960s. Liberalization will continue to create an increasingly open host economy for the operations of prospective investors. This holds true for land, manpower, general public sector efficiency, and relations with mainland China.

*Land, Manpower, Finance, and Public Sector Efficiency.* In July 1993, Taiwan's cabinet launched the Economic Revitalization Program, an action plan to promote private investment to develop Taiwan into an Asia-Pacific regional operations center and accelerate its industrial upgrading.

This program designated immediate action to remedy the shortages of land and manpower, to increase and improve technological resources, and to improve Taiwan's financial environment. Land programs include opening up land owned by the government and public enterprises, converting farmland to use by industry and public works, and accelerating the development of industrial zones. High-tech companies will enjoy a five-year exemption from the business income tax and will be offered tax credits to encourage plant and office automation. The plan also includes reform of government administration and government enterprises through laws, regulations, and other measures to modernize the civil service, install full administrative coordination, and improve the efficiency of government enterprises.

*Relations with Mainland China.* Taiwan's relations with mainland China have changed dramatically after half a century of military and political confrontation. The high degree of resource complementarity and division of labor and the fading of the cold war have encouraged the recent warming of relations across the Taiwan Strait. Increasing economic and trade exchanges between Taiwan and the mainland have become a strong trend that would be difficult to stop.

Taiwan's Economic Revitalization Program therefore calls for clear and realistic policies regarding cross-strait relations. It proposes a step-by-step relaxation of cross-strait exchange restrictions, support to Taiwan investors who invest in the mainland, promotion of cross-strait technological exchanges, and recruitment of mainland talent.

## Development Strategy

Taiwan's economic integration with the rest of the Asia-Pacific region is largely through the connections of influential Chinese communities spread throughout the economies of Taiwan, Hong Kong, Singapore, mainland China, other Southeast Asian states, and even Europe and the United States. These areas are thus prime sites for companies planning to start regional operations in Taiwan. As a center for regional operations, Taiwan must be equipped to provide sufficient infrastructure to advance the free mobility of goods, manpower, capital, services, and other resources for the successful performance of regional operations in these areas.

The Council for Economic Planning and Development, Executive Yuan, has studied the alternatives for Taiwan as a host to regional operations centers. According to the council's report, Taiwan can emphasize the development of regional operations centers in three directions: transportation, specialized services, and production centers.[23]

### Transportation Center

*Aviation.* An air transport center in Taiwan for passenger and express cargo flights would have the following advantages:

- a central location between Southeast and Northeast Asia and between mainland China and the American continent;
- direct and convenient routes linking major cities in the Asia-Pacific region;
- a domestic market sufficient to support basic demand for the service;
- efficient and high-quality transfer services;
- the flexibility to allow interested enterprises to operate with their own equipment and facilities;
- twenty-four hour operations;
- quick and efficient customs processing;
- adequate and smooth connecting lines.

The Taiwan government has been working aggressively to elevate Taiwan's overall technical capabilities and to establish an aerospace industrial infrastructure. The theme of this effort—"aerospace software-related technology transfer"—should promote technology transfer and build international business alliances and will certainly help build a firm base for the development of Taiwan as an air transport center.

***Marine Transport.***   A sea transport center in Taiwan can perform value-adding operations such as cargo transfer, warehousing, packaging, and delivery. Taiwan has the following qualifications to accommodate such a center:

- a central geographic position;
- fast and convenient lines with major ports in the Asia-Pacific region;
- fast processing of cargo transfer (for example, express customs processing);
- an environment that will permit many types of operations and self-ownership of docks.

## Specialized Service Center

***International Financial Center.***   Calls for creating an international financial center in Taiwan have been heard since liberalization began. Recently, Taiwan's Central Bank of China announced ambitious plans to make Taiwan a regional funding center by introducing new financial products, improving the market structure and system, and amending certain business laws. The bank hopes to incorporate a foreign exchange broker-age in Taipei and establish Taiwan's own system for foreign exchange price reporting.

The directorate-general of telecommunications, working with an institution that provides global financial market infor-mation, agreed with the CBC to introduce an instant global bond transaction system in September 1994. The CBC also proposed operating the gold market around the clock so that it is compati-ble with the gold markets in Europe and the United States. The Council for Economic Planning and Development has suggested that Taiwan develop offshore banking (for example, joint loan and mutual fund management), overseas investment support, and other international banking procedures. It cites three condi-tions for such development:

- a large-scale international trade and investment network;
- a liberal environment for operations;
- efficient financial institutions with highly skilled profes-sionals.

*Telecommunications Center.* A telecommunications center should be able to manage the exchange of international corre-spondence based on the following conditions:

- direct cable links between Taiwan and connecting coun-tries;
- competitive prices for international telephone service;
- reliable exchange stations and regional networks.

Network management is another logical function of a tele-communications center. Network management centers in Taiwan can provide communications networks and management ser-vices for international enterprises under the following condi-tions:

- high demand for business communications;
- high-quality private network services;
- competitive international network rental service.

*Media Center.* Based on the following advantages, Taiwan can be developed into a center for media production and broad-casting. As a media production center it would need to provide the following:

- an extensive market for Chinese-language programs;
- talented performers and good technicians;
- excellent media production hardware and software facilities, including camera studios, videotaping equipment, and production and distribution mechanisms.

A broadcasting and station production center must have the capability to organize and compile programs, advertise and market, and broadcast. Taiwan will have the edge if it has

- the ability to develop the market in mainland China;
- an unrestricted environment for production;
- the capacity to broadcast programs via satellite.

### Production Center

Taiwan can be developed into a production center to perform value-adding activities including product development, high-end parts production, and high-tech assembly as well as training, business management, and technical assistance relevant to all the activities connected with the production center.

To create a desirable environment for the operations of regional production centers in Taiwan, the following conditions are needed:

- a sufficient supply of skilled labor and sound industrial structure;
- extensive regional trade interdependence;
- low production costs (low land taxes, land prices, and interest rates as well as generous tax incentives);
- a buoyant local market.

***Manpower training.***   A regional manpower training center can be set up in Taiwan if the following conditions are met:

- easy entry and exit;
- a good training environment—readily available facilities, such as production plants, in which to conduct training;
- a competent training force (for example, teaching staff proficient in foreign languages).

***Technical assistance.***   A regional technical assistance center should have the technology to meet regional demand. Such an operations center will require the following:

- adequate technology for production and R&D;
- a reserve of science and technology talent;
- a sound environment and facilities for R&D.

***Business Management.*** A management center in Taiwan can support the management of regional branches if Taiwan can provide

- convenient regional transportation;
- an experienced managerial force;
- convenient entry and exit procedures for foreigners (for exam ple, to attend regional meetings).

# 7

# Taiwan's Role in the Asia-Pacific Region

The new world order is taking shape, and the Asia-Pacific region is forging a new economic order.

As Taiwan has become more closely integrated with other Asia-Pacific economies, it has had an effect on many regional issues. Besides its involvement in the economy of its own region, Taiwan has also succeeded to a considerable extent in engaging with other parts of the world. In this era of globalization and regional cooperation, Taiwan is ready to play an expanded role, with special emphasis on the Asia-Pacific economy.

## Asia-Pacific Economic Cooperation

During the Asia-Pacific region's current period of rapid and sustained growth, regional interaction and interdependence among individual economies have expanded tremendously.

New problems are also emerging.

With the rapid development in this region, these include trade frictions, labor migration, exchange rate adjustments, competition for economic resources and their development, harmonization between environmental conservation and economic expansion, and differing perceptions by industrial and less developed economies about what constitutes market openness. The need for consultation and cooperation on shaping new economic arrangements that address these issues in a cooperative spirit has become more and more apparent.

APEC began in 1989 as a loosely organized and consultative group, with members competing against one another for export markets and having unresolved political differences. In November 1993, however, the economic and political leaders of APEC's member states held an unprecedented meeting, followed by a second meeting in November 1994. During these meetings, the leaders and ministers who attended demonstrated a commitment to free trade, to combining the energy of their diverse economies, and to promoting sustained prosperity. Because they recognize the open multilateral trading system as the vital conduit of economic growth, all APEC members are likely to form an open rather than a defensive bloc. APEC members also possess an entrepreneurial spirit and market-oriented policies in their individual economies. Economic liberalization is likely to be strengthened in each domestic economy, and cooperation in investment, trade, and harmonization of standards will increase.

APEC economies have encountered a number of development challenges following an extended period of rapid growth. Growth in industrial countries is slowing due to a prolonged economic adjustment process. Meanwhile, developing countries are facing problems of inadequate physical infrastructure—electricity, water supply, telecommunications, and transportation—and of underdeveloped institutional structures and regulatory frameworks. Ensuring noninflationary growth, financing investment and infrastructural development, and promoting capital market development will all appear on the APEC agenda.

Taiwan attaches great importance to its active membership in APEC. Taiwan's economic achievements are due largely to its continuous pursuit of economic liberalization and closer economic relations with other Asia-Pacific countries. These efforts have created enormous trade and investment opportunities for the people of Taiwan, enabling the economy to continue its growth and progress. As the economy has matured, it has fed back the benefits of growth into the regional economy. Taiwan's continuing growth in foreign trade, overseas investment, and employment of foreign workers have made a considerable contribution to regional economic development.

In the last decade of the twentieth century, Taiwan has made further liberalization and internationalization its top economic priorities. It has the opportunity and responsibility to share with other APEC members the rich experience it has accumulated during its transformation from a developing economy to an NIE as well as restructuring the economy in the process of liberalization.

Under the auspices of APEC, there are many cooperative programs such as the APEC Education Program and APEC Business Volunteer Program that Taiwan zealously supports. Taiwan already operates an Overseas Cooperation and Development Fund, which was set up to provide economic assistance and foster development in APEC countries or elsewhere.

Taiwan understands that market economies and free trade have brought prosperity to the Asia-Pacific region. It acknowledges with other APEC members the need to promote further trade liberalization and investment internationalization. The economies of APEC members are at different stages of development, and they have different concerns related to their particular circumstances. Taiwan has called for a flexibility that respects and accommodates such diversity by making cooperative efforts in technology transfer, resource development, and market opening.

Faithful to the global free trade system, Taiwan fully supports the goal of open regionalism. This demands that all regional arrangements be made in harmony with GATT principles and be open for all countries in the region to join on an equal basis. Taiwan envisions becoming both the proponent and the model for world trade liberalization and international cooperation.

## Taiwan's Deepening Economic Integration with the Region

Taiwan's industrial production is efficiently connected with both developed countries such as the United States and Japan and recently rising Asian developing economies such as mainland China and Southeast Asian countries. The impetus behind this integration is the spread and deepening of offshore direct investment by Taiwan businesses, the exodus from Taiwan of traditional labor-intensive production, and the swift industrial restructuring Taiwan has undergone since the late 1980s. Following the principle of division of labor in manufacturing high-tech goods, the United States and Japan supply raw materials and intermediate goods that are assembled and processed by Taiwan's relatively low-cost skilled labor into more sophisticated or higher-value-added products to be shipped to the industrial countries. In the production of conventional lower-tech, labor-intensive goods, Taiwan supplies machinery and intermediate materials that are assembled by low-cost unskilled labor in mainland China and Southeast Asia for export to the industrial countries.

Since it began reform and adopted an open policy in the beginning of the 1990s, Vietnam has become an attractive site for foreign investment. Because rapid economic expansion in the ASEAN-4 has generated upward pressure on prices and wages and has revealed inadequate infrastructure, Taiwan's overseas investment has begun a gradual shift from ASEAN to Vietnam.

Thousands of Taiwan manufacturing companies have moved their production lines wholly or partly abroad in recent years, but the manufacturing sector at home remains strong, growing steadily as domestic industry develops its niche in the regional economy. To maintain this trend, Taiwan needs new investment from both domestic and foreign sources. The government has sought to keep Taiwan attractive to investors while it implements the Economic Revitalization Plan. As described earlier, the government plan will upgrade industries, promote closer links with other Asia-Pacific economies, and upgrade technological expertise and infrastructure.

Foreign investors considering investment in Taiwan will focus on the rest of the region as well as on Taiwan. Because Taiwan is making an all-out effort to strengthen its regional role by fostering the most favorable environment in which to host regional operations for international competitors, investors may conclude that establishing regional operations centers in Taiwan is the best way to take advantage of Taiwan's position in the booming regional economy. A few international companies have already established their Asia-Pacific regional operations centers in Taiwan, and many others are getting ready to move in this direction. Proposals have come from companies in aviation, telecommunications, and wholesale industries; they include the formation of repair and maintenance, purchasing, and other regional operations centers.

## Future Regional Developments

More than 10 regional trade bodies have been established worldwide, of which the EU is the most successful. Although East Asia has been the fastest growing region of the world over the past 10 years, it has developed no formal and effective regional arrangements for cooperative economic organization. This situation highlights an interesting yet important fact: a legitimate trade integrating body is not necessarily the premise for rapid trade development, nor does its existence necessarily mean it can effectively promote trade.

Observation of the development of individual economies reveals a common feature: outward orientation. Trade has been the engine of growth for East Asian economies with almost no exception. Whether the analysis is a cross-section study among countries or a time-series analysis of a specific country, studies indicate that openness helps speed growth. Even the adjustment efforts of Japan and Taiwan to remedy their unusual external imbalances have increased their ties with other members of the Asia-Pacific region and helped promote the region's economic integration.

One can reason from the above that economic openness benefits development and that industrial division of labor within a region is good for the region's development. Japan led the way in the region's economic dynamism in the 1960s, followed by the four "little dragons" in the 1970s, the near-NIEs in Southeast Asia in the late 1980s, and mainland China and Indonesia more recently. These countries collectively have established an exemplary model for international specialization and division of labor. Soon Vietnam, Myanmar, and the Philippines will join the procession.

Economic integration of the Asia-Pacific region may face possible challenges from both mainland China's attitude toward openness and conflicts that disrupt international cooperation.

Within mainland China there exist vast ethnic and economic disparities that determine the varying pace and sequence of economic development and, thus, the various stages of development. In other words, some division of labor and specialization that are usually spread among a few smaller countries could all occur within the mainland's economy itself. This means that mainland China must develop complementary rather than opposing relations between external and internal approaches. Keeping the proper balance will be one of the mainland's great tasks.

As individual Asian countries forge ahead, competition among them will arise in spite of efforts at integration and cooperation. This rivalry will generate external as well as internal, yet manageable, tensions and instability. Since the 1980s, Japan, Taiwan, the United States, mainland China, Thailand, and South Korea have all experienced disorder and periods of adjustment. It is reasonable to assume this pattern will be repeated again and again.

# 8

# Conclusion

During the past three decades, Taiwan has created one of the world's greatest economic success stories, achieving rapid growth and industrialization in a stable environment. Since the mid-1980s, Taiwan's burgeoning economic strength has rectified its domestic imbalances and has made a constructive contribution to the Asia-Pacific region's integration.

Taiwan anticipates the establishment of three dominant economic groupings—Europe, North America, and East Asia—in a more open world economy that allows freer flows of commodities, capital, and labor. The future shape of world trade will depend in part on the past—for example, on how comparative advantage is affected by transportation costs or by geographic proximity. But with the far more intensive intraregional flows of the elements of production and quickly expanding global operations by multinational corporations, future world trading patterns will depend in larger part on the pursuit of regionalization and globalization. Taiwan's economic development during the last three decades has been a clear example of how a domestic economy evolves with external changes: Taiwan has gained continuously by emphasizing division of labor and economic liberalization, extrapolating from the foreign sector to the entire economy. Taiwan is now ready to fully embrace GATT consistency on the one hand and to develop physical infrastructure on the other, an approach that should yield respectable growth and greater economic welfare over the long run.

As one looks at growing regionalism, particularly in East Asia, the expanding role of Taiwan in the region is clear. Taiwan has become an economic nexus: it has combined its capital, technology, skilled labor, and managerial expertise with the rich natural resources, low-cost labor, and abundant land of the near-NIEs to produce the best of comparative advantages. To enhance this synergy, Taiwan has been eager to promote more formal integration of the region through active participation in APEC and other Asia-Pacific programs.

Despite complementary economic relations among Asia-Pacific economies, competition for regional resources and market shares is likely to arise. Multinationals, large and small, have spread throughout the region and constantly seek the most favorable location. Although complementarity among different regions may serve as the first driving force behind the relocation of production sites, competition among investors, local and foreign, in the host and source economies is bound to intensify. Complementarity is vital to attracting foreign investment in the short run, but the atmosphere of competition is more important in the long run. Competition among countries will add to the pressure on policymakers and may serve as the catalyst for national reform and upgrading and provide a more favorable environment for business operators. Subsequently, it will improve the performance of enterprises, resulting in greater prosperity and enhanced welfare for the region's inhabitants.

As Asia-Pacific countries harvest the benefits of free trade, they are likely to continue to advocate open policies, although obstacles to market access need to be resolved. The region has demonstrated great success so far in market-driven integration of member economies. But regional integration does not fall exactly within the framework of the WTO, which was established on January 1, 1995, to implement the Uruguay Round accords that are expected to boost global income by more than $200 billion in the next 10 years.

Unlike trade blocs in Europe and North America, which have been formed according to traditional relationships and promoted by institutional arrangement, the East Asian trade group has emerged primarily because of market forces and in spite of the diversified economic, political, and cultural backgrounds of member economies. Despite the challenge from the European and North American blocs, the Asia-Pacific region seems to be under no pressure to change its present pattern of economic integration, which has been a praiseworthy model of "open regionalism." Taiwan is prepared to play an active and constructive role in this direction to promote both its own interests and those of the region.

The following developments will shape this role for Taiwan:

- The Asia-Pacific region is becoming the world's economic center of gravity. Economic interdependence in the region is deepening despite the absence of a political framework for regional consolidation.

- Mainland China is confirming its commitment to the market economy regardless of how it characterizes that commitment. The mainland's economy has been growing at 8.8 percent per annum since 1978, perhaps unprecedented for an economy of its size.
- Taiwan has been investing heavily in both mainland China and Southeast Asia, ensuring Taiwan's regional role in the emerging Asia-Pacific economy.
- NAFTA has been formed and might be expanded in the future.
- The Uruguay Round talks have successfully concluded and the agreements implemented.

Taiwan is expecting to enter the new world trade body, and international companies will be drawn to Taiwan because of its increasing openness and opportunities in both Taiwan and the region as a whole. Taiwan's already existing links with both the regional economy and the industrial economies, combined with Taiwan's new openness and opportunities, could make Taiwan the best location for a hub within the region. Although thousands of Taiwan manufacturing companies have moved their production lines abroad in recent years, the manufacturing sector remains strong and continues steady growth as it discovers new niches in the regional economy. And Taiwan is making an all-out effort to assume the role of regional operations center by fostering the most favorable environment for international competitors.

Today, foreign investors coming to Taiwan are focusing not only on the future of Taiwan but on that of the region as a whole and on mainland China in particular. Reforms in mainland China have opened that vast economy to the outside world and especially to Taiwan, despite decades-old mutual enmity. As investors the world over are drawn to mainland China's unexploited market, Taiwan has been a significant middleman between the mainland and the world outside. The economy of the mainland will develop additional links with Taiwan if political and economic reforms continue. Foreign interest in the mainland hinges on the extent of openness and of any instability that accompanies the mainland's reform efforts. For Taiwan, this means making an even greater effort to detach political issues with the mainland from economic affairs. It is reasonable to hope that in the future the mainland will also concentrate on economic development and the prosperity of its people. If economic relations dominate cross-strait ties, the regional and global benefits of a regional operations center in Taiwan can be fully realized.

Over the past decade, economic development has significantly improved the standard of living in the Asia-Pacific region. The most important development has been the creation of a dynamic atmosphere for widespread growth in the region. Despite inevitable trade conflicts and industrial restructuring, the region's social stability has been enhanced. Governments in the region must continue, of course, to pay attention to interregional as well as intraregional disparities in development in such areas as income distribution and technology development. These are formidable challenges for Taiwan and other economies in the coming decade, and regional economic cooperation among the economies in this region certainly goes beyond relationships determined only by market forces.

# Notes

1.   All dollar amounts stated in this monograph are U.S. dollars unless designated otherwise.

2.   Newly industrializing economies (NIEs) are that subgroup of developing countries that has experienced particularly rapid economic growth. Asia's newly industrializing economies, also known as the Four Dragons, are Hong Kong, South Korea, Singapore, and Taiwan.

3.   The Association of Southeast Asian Nations, better known as ASEAN, was established in August 1967. Its six members are Brunei, Indonesia, Malaysia, the Philippines, Singapore, and Thailand.

4.   International Monetary Fund, *Direction of Trade Statistics Yearbook, 1993* (Washington, D.C.: IMF, 1994). Asian developing countries include the NIEs, ASEAN excluding Singapore, mainland China, Afghanistan, Bangladesh, Cambodia, Fiji, French Polynesia, Guam, India, Kiribati, North Korea, Laos, Macao, Maldives, Myanmar, Nepal, New Caledonia, Pakistan, Papua New Guinea, American Samoa, Solomon Islands, Sri Lanka, Tonga, Tuvalu, Vanuatu, Vietnam, and Western Samoa.

5.   The ASEAN-4 is composed of Indonesia, Malaysia, the Philippines, and Thailand.

6.   United Nations statistics show that FDI had increased from $2.3 billion to $4.4 billion between 1987 and 1991 in mainland China and from $1.5 billion to $8.1 billion in the ASEAN countries except Singapore. United Nations, *World Investment Report, 1993* (New York, 1994).

7.   The Group of Seven, or G-7, is composed of Canada, France, Germany, Italy, Japan, the United Kingdom, and the United States.

8.   The Group of Five, or G-5, is composed of France, Germany, Japan, the United Kingdom, and the United States.

9.   The comparison of unit labor cost, standardized in terms of the U.S. dollar, allows for adjustments and variations in the exchange rate, the wage rate, and labor productivity. Figures are based on 1982=100.

10.   For a more detailed analysis, see Chi Schive, "How Did Taiwan Solve its Dutch Disease Problem?" in *Research in Asian Economic Studies*, vol. 5 of *Asia-Pacific Economies: 1990s and Beyond* (London, England: JAI Press, 1994), 183–202.

11.   Chi Schive, "Cross-Investment in the Asia-Pacific: Taiwan's Inward and Outward Investment," *Business and the Contemporary World* 5, no. 2 (spring 1993): 89–104.

**12.** Statistics Department, Ministry of Economic Affairs (MOEA), Taipei, *Manufacturing Investment Survey,* June 1994 (in Chinese).

**13.** Investment Commission, Ministry of Economic Affairs, Taipei, *Statistics on Outward Technical Cooperation, 1993* (in Chinese).

**14.** P. K. Chiang, "Taiwan's Economic Development: Its Path, Challenges, and Strategies," *Industry of Free China* 82, no. 1 (1994) (in Chinese).

**15.** Although cross-strait trade estimates compiled by Hong Kong customs have been far lower than the actual statistics, these data are used in this section to keep a consistent base for comparison. For example, Taiwan's exports to the mainland totaled $7.6 billion according to Hong Kong customs, but the closer estimate is $14.0 billion. The difference is attributable to illegal shipments and transfers and transmodal shipments that are not required to report to Hong Kong customs.

**16.** Lin argues that intra-industry trade within the manufacturing sector did not become noticeable until 1985, when Taiwan's manufacturing industries started to invest heavily in the mainland, and neither vertical nor horizontal specialization of cross-strait trade has demonstrated a steady trend. Yuh-Jiun Nancy Lin, "Comparison Analysis of Taiwan's Intra-industry Trade with Mainland China and other Trading Partners," Chung-Hua Institution for Economic Research, Taipei, 1994 (in Chinese).

**17.** Research conducted by the Chung-Hua Institution for Economic Research for the Council for Economic Planning and Development draws this conclusion by using data for 1990. Tzong-Ta Yen, "Investment in and Trade with the Mainland by Taiwan Businessmen," Chung-Hua Institution for Economic Research, Taipei, 1992 (in Chinese).

**18.** Chi Schive, "Direct Foreign Investment and Linkage Effects: The Experience of Taiwan," *Canadian Journal of Development Studies* 11, no. 2 (1990): 325–341.

**19.** Investment Commission, Ministry of Economic Affairs, Taipei, *Report on Investment by Taiwan and Foreign Businesses in the Mainland,* June 1994 (in Chinese).

**20.** Chi Schive, "Hong Kong's Role in Cross-Strait Economic Contacts and Issues of Direct Cross-Strait Transportation Links," Council for Economic Planning and Development, Taipei, 1994 (internal paper) (in Chinese).

**21.** *Direction of Trade Statistics Yearbook, 1993,* p.5.

**22.** International Institute for Management Development, Lausanne, Switzerland, *World Competitiveness Report,* 1992.

**23.** Council for Economic Planning and Development, Taipei, *Feasibility Report on Taiwan as a Regional Operations Center,* forthcoming (in Chinese).

# Tables

**Table 3.1**
**External Imbalance in Taiwan's Economy, 1980–1993**
(in percentages)

| Year | Exports /GNP (1) | Imports /GNP (2) | External imbalance as share of GNP (1) – (2) |
|------|------|------|------|
| 1980 | 52.6 | 53.8 | 1.2 |
| 1981 | 52.2 | 50.2 | 2.0 |
| 1982 | 50.2 | 45.0 | 5.2 |
| 1983 | 53.0 | 44.4 | 8.6 |
| 1984 | 55.6 | 44.5 | 11.1 |
| 1985 | 53.3 | 39.8 | 13.5 |
| 1986 | 56.7 | 37.4 | 19.3 |
| 1987 | 56.4 | 39.3 | 13.1 |
| 1988 | 53.4 | 41.6 | 11.8 |
| 1989 | 49.2 | 41.2 | 8.0 |
| 1990 | 46.6 | 40.7 | 5.9 |
| 1991 | 47.3 | 42.4 | 4.9 |
| 1992 | 43.6 | 41.2 | 2.4 |
| 1993 | 44.6 | 42.7 | 1.9 |

*Source:* Directorate-General of Budget, Accounting and Statistics, Executive Yuan, Taipei, *Quarterly National Economic Trends, Taiwan Area, The Republic of China*, various issues.

**Table 3.2**
**Index of Unit Labor Cost Changes in U.S. Dollars,**
**Selected Countries, 1980–1991**
(1982 = 100)

| Year | Taiwan | Japan | South Korea | United States | West Germany |
|------|--------|-------|-------------|---------------|--------------|
| 1980 | 87  | 107 | 104 | 87  | 124 |
| 1981 | 97  | 114 | 100 | 94  | 104 |
| 1982 | 100 | 100 | 100 | 100 | 100 |
| 1983 | 97  | 103 | 94  | 98  | 95  |
| 1984 | 108 | 99  | 90  | 96  | 86  |
| 1985 | 112 | 97  | 88  | 97  | 85  |
| 1986 | 127 | 142 | 83  | 97  | 120 |
| 1987 | 160 | 157 | 91  | 94  | 156 |
| 1988 | 170 | 173 | 112 | 92  | 160 |
| 1989 | 192 | 161 | 153 | 93  | 150 |
| 1990 | 199 | -   | 160 | -   | -   |
| 1991 | 200 | -   | 163 | -   | -   |

*Sources:*   U.S. Department of Labor, Bureau of Labor Statistics, Washington, D.C., *Monthly Labor Review,* various issues; Directorate-General of Budget, Accounting and Statistics, Executive Yuan, Taipei, *Monthly Bulletin of Earnings and Productivity Statistics*, various issues.

## Table 3.3
## Automation in Taiwan's Manufacturing Sector, 1981–1991

**Ratio of automatic machinery over total**
(in percentages)

| Year | Foods | Textiles | Plastic products | Machinery | Electronics |
|------|-------|----------|------------------|-----------|-------------|
| 1981 | -     | 29       | 8                | 21        | 27          |
| 1983 | 66    | 24       | 10               | 28        | 38          |
| 1985 | 56    | 55       | 26               | 36        | 46          |
| 1987 | 73    | 65       | 41               | 55        | 59          |

**Automatic machinery per worker**
(New Taiwan[NT]$ million/person)

| Year | Foods | Textiles | Plastic products | Machinery | Electronics |
|------|-------|----------|------------------|-----------|-------------|
| 1985 | 20.3  | 28.4     | 13.1             | 36.0      | 15.8        |
| 1987 | 35.7  | 36.9     | 20.5             | 34.9      | 24.1        |
| 1989 | 29.1  | 64.1     | 57.4             | 34.7      | 31.0        |
| 1991 | 83.2  | 79.6     | 51.7             | 60.3      | 61.6        |

*Sources:* Automation Commission, Executive Yuan, Taipei, *Industrial Automation, A Survey Report (1982, 1984, 1986 and 1988 )*; Ministry of Economic Affairs, Taipei, *Industrial Automation Survey Report*, June 1993.

*Note:* Automatic machinery denotes machinery that can operate within a work period without requiring the attention of a worker.

## Table 3.4
## Taiwan's Exports by Technology Level, 1983–1993
(in percentages)

| Year | Technology Intensity | | Heavy industries | High-tech products |
|------|------|------|------|------|
| | High | Medium and low | | |
| 1983 | 18.2 | 81.8 | 35.4 | 26.0 |
| 1984 | 18.3 | 81.7 | 36.4 | 27.2 |
| 1985 | 18.8 | 81.2 | 36.5 | 27.0 |
| 1986 | 18.4 | 81.6 | 35.6 | 27.6 |
| 1987 | 19.4 | 80.6 | 37.9 | 30.0 |
| 1988 | 22.6 | 77.4 | 42.8 | 33.7 |
| 1989 | 24.2 | 75.8 | 44.5 | 33.9 |
| 1990 | 26.7 | 73.3 | 46.7 | 35.9 |
| 1991 | 27.2 | 72.8 | 46.7 | 36.3 |
| 1992 | 29.5 | 70.5 | 49.1 | 37.9 |
| 1993 | - | - | 51.9 | 41.6 |

*Source:* Ministry of Finance, Taipei, *Monthly Statistics of Exports and Imports, Taiwan Area,* March 1994.

**Table 3.5**
**Taiwan's Exports by Industry Classification, 1981–1993**
(in percentages)

| | 1981 | 1982 | 1983 | 1984 | 1985 | 1986 | 1987 | 1988 | 1989 | 1990 | 1991 | 1992 | 1993 |
|---|---|---|---|---|---|---|---|---|---|---|---|---|---|
| Agriculture, forestry, fishery, livestock, and hunting products | 2.69 | 2.28 | 2.17 | 1.97 | 1.76 | 1.68 | 1.40 | 1.61 | 0.96 | 0.84 | 0.91 | 0.87 | 0.86 |
| Processed food | 4.90 | 5.18 | 4.61 | 4.03 | 4.32 | 4.72 | 4.54 | 3.75 | 3.58 | 3.52 | 3.62 | 3.31 | 3.57 |
| Beverage and tobacco preparation | 0.1 | 0.1 | 0.1 | 0.0 | 0.04 | 0.03 | 0.03 | 0.04 | 0.03 | 0.03 | 0.05 | 0.06 | 0.07 |
| Energy and minerals | 0.1 | 0.0 | 0.0 | 0.0 | 0.08 | 0.06 | 0.11 | 0.07 | 0.06 | 0.05 | 0.04 | 0.04 | 0.07 |
| Construction materials | 0.44 | 0.66 | 0.77 | 0.55 | 0.50 | 0.40 | 0.32 | 0.32 | 0.27 | 0.28 | 0.23 | 0.22 | 0.18 |
| Intermediate goods: | | | | | | | | | | | | | |
| A[a] | 9.92 | 10.44 | 9.51 | 9.09 | 8.73 | 7.45 | 6.90 | 8.77 | 8.99 | 9.49 | 9.45 | 9.45 | 11.07 |
| B[b] | 26.53 | 25.28 | 25.90 | 25.59 | 26.99 | 26.19 | 26.66 | 27.79 | 31.07 | 34.99 | 37.00 | 39.11 | 37.76 |
| Consumer nondurable goods | 35.27 | 35.56 | 36.14 | 36.81 | 35.85 | 35.61 | 33.48 | 29.77 | 27.46 | 23.72 | 21.95 | 19.79 | 18.09 |
| Consumer durable goods | 11.90 | 11.13 | 11.61 | 11.03 | 9.08 | 11.01 | 11.42 | 10.08 | 10.16 | 8.70 | 8.52 | 7.95 | 8.23 |
| Machinery | 6.16 | 6.16 | 6.93 | 9.03 | 10.39 | 10.93 | 13.21 | 15.42 | 15.45 | 16.34 | 16.11 | 17.24 | 17.51 |
| Transportation equipment | 1.90 | 2.99 | 1.90 | 1.63 | 1.72 | 1.87 | 1.87 | 1.54 | 1.89 | 2.11 | 2.12 | 1.96 | 2.59 |

*Source:* Ministry of Finance, Taipei, *Report on the Characteristic Classifications of Tradable Commodities*, 1993.
*Note:* Industry classification follows World Bank scheme. See Bela Balassa and Associates, *Development Strategies in Semi-industrial Economies* (Baltimore, MD: The Johns Hopkins University Press, 1982).
[a] Intermediate products A are products that can be used for consumer goods or producer goods after processing.
[b] Intermediate products B are products that can be used for consumer goods or producer goods without processing.

**Table 4.1**
**Taiwan's Outward Investment by Region and Industry, 1993**
(in thousands of U.S. dollars)

| | Asia | Americas | Europe | Oceania | Africa | Total |
|---|---|---|---|---|---|---|
| Food and beverage processing | 14,379 | - | - | - | - | 14,379 |
| Textiles | 86,556 | 220 | - | - | - | 86,776 |
| Garments and footwear | 8,560 | - | - | - | - | 8,560 |
| Leather and fur products | 554 | - | - | - | - | 554 |
| Lumber and bamboo products | 2,633 | 11,154 | - | - | - | 13,787 |
| Paper products and printing | 110,054 | 450 | - | - | - | 110,504 |
| Chemicals | 34,704 | 275,640 | - | - | - | 310,344 |
| Rubber products | 91 | - | - | - | - | 91 |
| Non-metallic minerals | 22,900 | 946 | - | - | - | 23,846 |
| Base metals and metal products | 18,161 | 2,000 | 291 | - | 415 | 20,867 |
| Machinery equipment | 1,038 | - | - | - | - | 1,038 |
| Electronic and electric appliances | 62,188 | 18,995 | 23,056 | - | - | 104,239 |
| Trade | 83,782 | 42,353 | 170,370 | 63 | - | 296,568 |
| Transportation | 14,000 | 10,000 | 9,584 | - | - | 33,584 |
| Banking and insurance | 155,215 | 295,548 | 800 | 200 | - | 451,763 |
| Services | 5,702 | 16,631 | 44,000 | 720 | - | 67,053 |
| Other | 42,997 | 65,673 | 7,812 | 0 | 0 | 116,482 |
| **Total** | **663,514** | **739,610** | **255,913** | **983** | **415** | **1,660,435** |

*Source:* Investment Commission, Ministry of Economic Affairs, Taipei, *Statistics on Outward Investment*, various issues.
*Note:* Figures exclude Taiwan's investment in mainland China.

**Table 4.2**
**Taiwan's Outward Investment by Region, 1952–1993**
(in thousands of U.S. dollars)

| Year | Asia | Americas | Europe | Oceania | Africa | Total |
|------|------|----------|--------|---------|--------|-------|
| 1952–1979 | 43,057 | 13,576 | 142 | 2,074 | 441 | 59,290 |
| 1980 | 3,170 | 35,130 | 1,000 | 2,781 | 24 | 42,105 |
| 1981 | 6,738 | 1,795 | 2,231 | - | - | 10,764 |
| 1982 | 9,132 | 2,500 | - | - | - | 11,632 |
| 1983 | 6,561 | 2,858 | - | 144 | 1,000 | 10,563 |
| 1984 | 6,551 | 32,178 | - | 134 | 400 | 39,263 |
| 1985 | 4,206 | 35,830 | 891 | 7 | 400 | 41,334 |
| 1986 | 8,412 | 46,738 | 194 | 717 | 850 | 56,911 |
| 1987 | 21,302 | 80,250 | 199 | - | 1,000 | 102,751 |
| 1988 | 69,299 | 130,335 | 12,005 | 6,134 | 963 | 218,736 |
| 1989 | 296,372 | 624,431 | 2,333 | - | 7,850 | 930,986 |
| 1990 | 602,910 | 838,711 | 96,176 | 1,397 | 13,012 | 1,552,206 |
| 1991 | 929,819 | 658,958 | 60,289 | 2,441 | 4,523 | 1,656,030 |
| 1992 | 369,929 | 449,096 | 45,933 | 5,426 | 16,875 | 887,259 |
| 1993 | 663,514 | 739,610 | 255,913 | 983 | 415 | 1,660,435 |

*Source:* Investment Commission, Ministry of Economic Affairs, Taipei, *Statistics on Outward Investment,* various issues.

*Note:* Figures exclude Taiwan's investment in mainland China.

**Table 4.3**
**Taiwan's Investment in ASEAN and Mainland China, 1959–1993**
(in millions of U.S. dollars and number of projects)

| Year | Thailand | | Malaysia | | Philippines | | Indonesia | | Mainland China (Contract basis) |
|---|---|---|---|---|---|---|---|---|---|
| | Taiwan approved | Local approved | Taiwan approved | Local approved | Taiwan approved | Local approved | Taiwan approved | Local approved | |
| 1959–1986 | 15.2 (29) | 577.5 (157) | 7.3 (19) | 50.4 (138) | 27.5 (12) | 7.8 (54) | 10.1 (1) | 170.0 (3) | – |
| 1987 | 5.4 (5) | 307.6 (102) | 5.8 (5) | 91.0 (37) | 2.6 (3) | 9.0 (43) | 1.0 (1) | 8.4 (3) | 100.0 (80) |
| 1988 | 11.9 (15) | 859.9 (308) | 2.7 (5) | 313.0 (111) | 36.2 (7) | 109.9 (86) | 1.9 (3) | 913.0 (17) | 420.0 (355) |
| 1989 | 51.6 (23) | 892.2 (214) | 158.6 (25) | 815.0 (191) | 6 (13) | 148.7 (190) | 148.7 (1) | 158.0 (50) | 517.0 (547) |
| 1990 | 149.4 (39) | 782.7 (144) | 184.9 (36) | 2,383.0 (270) | 123.6 (16) | 140.7 (158) | 61.9 (18) | 618.3 (94) | 984.0 (1,117) |

**Table 4.3 (continued)**
**Taiwan's Investment in ASEAN and Mainland China, 1959–1993**
(in millions of U.S. dollars and number of projects)

| Year | Thailand | | Malaysia | | Philippines | | Indonesia | | Mainland China (Contract basis) |
| --- | --- | --- | --- | --- | --- | --- | --- | --- | --- |
| | Taiwan approved | Local approved | Taiwan approved | Local approved | Taiwan approved | Local approved | Taiwan approved | Local approved | |
| 1991 | 86.4 | 583.5 | 442.0 | 1,314.2 | 1.3 | 11.6 | 160.3 | 1,056.5 | 1,392.3 |
| | (33) | (69) | (35) | (182) | (2) | (109) | (25) | (57) | (1,735) |
| 1992 | 83.3 | 289.9 | 155.7 | 602 | 1.2 | 9.3 | 39.9 | 563.3 | 5,547.9 |
| | (23) | (44) | (13) | (137) | (3) | (27) | (20) | (23) | (6,430) |
| 1993 | 109.2 | 215.0 | 64.5 | 346.5 | 6.5 | 5.4 | 25.5 | 131.4 | 9,965.0 |
| | (19) | (61) | (18) | (86) | (12) | (21) | (11) | (21) | (10,948) |

*Sources:* Investment Commission, Ministry of Economic Affairs, Taipei, *Statistics on Outward Investment*, various issues; Board of Investment (BOI), Thailand; Malaysian Industrial Development Authority (MIDA), Malaysia; Board of Investment (BOI), the Philippines; Badan Koordinasi Penanaman Modal (BKPM) [Investment Coordinating Board], Indonesia; State Commission for Cooperation and Investment (SCCI), Vietnam.

*Notes:* ASEAN excluding Singapore and Brunei.
The numbers in ( ) beneath the dollar amounts denote the number of projects.

**Table 4.4**
**Taiwan's Investment in ASEAN and Vietnam, with Ranking and Major Industries of Interest**
(Approved by Host Countries, 1959–1993)

| | Singapore | Malaysia | Thailand | Indonesia | Philippines | Vietnam |
|---|---|---|---|---|---|---|
| Amount (U.S.$ 100 million) | 0.9 | 59.2 | 45.1 | 36.2 | 4.4 | 15.3 |
| Number of projects | 62 | 1,152 | 1,099 | 268 | 688 | 117 |
| Ranking among all investing countries in the host country | 13 | 2 | 4 | 3 | 5 | 1 |
| Countries with higher ranking | Japan United States others | Japan | Japan Hong Kong United States | Japan Hong Kong | United States Japan Hong Kong United Kingdom | |

**Table 4.4 (continued)**
**Taiwan's Investment in ASEAN and Vietnam, with Ranking and Major Industries of Interest**
(Approved by Host Countries, 1959–1993)

| | Singapore | Malaysia | Thailand | Indonesia | Philippines | Vietnam |
|---|---|---|---|---|---|---|
| Major industries of interest | 1. Textiles | 1. Electronic and electrical products | 1. Machinery hardware | 1. Pulp and paper | 1. Textiles | 1. Footwear |
| | 2. Electronic and electrical products | 2. Textiles | 2. Electronics and telecommunications | 2. Textiles | 2. Electronic and electrical products | 2. Food |
| | 3. Garments | 3. Rubber products | 3. Plastics and rubber | 3. Agriculture | 3. Rubber and plastic products | 3. Construction |
| | 4. Plastic Processing | 4. Wood and woodworks | 4. Textiles | 4. Metal products | 4. Food | 4. Textiles |
| | 5. Non-ferrous metals | 5. Alloy forging | 5. Chemicals | 5. Chemicals | | 5. Construction |

*Sources:* Board of Investment (BOI), Thailand; Malaysian Industrial Development Authority (MIDA), Malaysia; Board of Investment (BOI), the Philippines; Badan Koordinasi Penanaman Modal (BKPM) [Investment Coordinating Board], Indonesia; Economic Development Board (EDB), Singapore; State Commission for Cooperation and Investment (SCCI), Vietnam.

*Note:* ASEAN excluding Brunei.

**Table 4.5**
**Taiwan's Investment in ASEAN and Vietnam, Approved by Host Countries, 1959–1993**
(in millions of U.S. dollars and number of projects)

| Year | Thailand $ | No. | Malaysia $ | No. | Philippines $ | No. | Indonesia $ | No. | Singapore $ | No. | Vietnam $ | No. |
|---|---|---|---|---|---|---|---|---|---|---|---|---|
| 1959–1986 | 577.45 | 157 | 50.39 | 138 | 7.82 | 54 | 170.00 | 3 | 61.62 | 48 | | |
| 1987 | 307.58 | 102 | 91.00 | 37 | 9.04 | 43 | 8.40 | 3 | 0.01 | 1 | | |
| 1988 | 859.94 | 308 | 313.00 | 111 | 109.87 | 86 | 913.00 | 17 | 0.67 | 3 | 0.00[a] | 0[a] |
| 1989 | 892.20 | 214 | 815.00 | 191 | 148.69 | 190 | 158.00 | 50 | 0.54 | 1 | 1.00 | 1 |
| 1990 | 782.69 | 144 | 2,383.00 | 270 | 140.65 | 158 | 618.30 | 94 | 3.16 | 3 | 104.43 | 18 |
| 1991 | 583.46 | 69 | 1,314.21 | 182 | 11.61 | 109 | 1,056.50 | 57 | 23.73 | 4 | 457.66 | 28 |
| 1992 | 289.92 | 44 | 602.00 | 137 | 9.27 | 27 | 563.30 | 23 | 0.19 | 1 | 531.41 | 23 |
| 1993 | 215.00 | 61 | 346.50 | 86 | 5.37 | 21 | 131.40 | 21 | 0.25 | 1 | 436.54 | 47 |
| **Subtotal** | **4,508.24** | **1,099** | **5,915.10** | **1,152** | **442.32** | **688** | **3,618.90** | **268** | **90.17** | **62** | **1,531.04** | **117** |

**Total amount: U.S.$   16,105.77 million**
**Total number of projects:   3,386**

*Sources:*   Board of Investment (BOI), Thailand; Malaysian Industrial Development Authority (MIDA), Malaysia; Board of Investment (BOI), the Philippines; Badan Koordinasi Penanaman Modal (BKPM) [Investment Coordinating Board], Indonesia; Economic Development Board (EDB), Singapore; State Commission for Cooperation and Investment (SCCI), Vietnam.

*Note:*   ASEAN excluding Brunei.

[a] For years 1959-1988.

**Table 4.6**
**Taiwan's Outward Investment by Industry, 1952–1993**
(in thousands of U.S. dollars)

| | 1952-1979 | 1980 | 1981 | 1982 | 1983 | 1984 | 1985 | 1986 |
|---|---|---|---|---|---|---|---|---|
| Food and beverage processing | 7,730 | 240 | - | - | - | - | 2,250 | - |
| Textiles | 3,486 | 24 | - | 7,000 | - | 170 | - | - |
| Garments and footwear | 749 | - | - | - | - | 426 | 400 | 800 |
| Leather and fur products | - | - | - | - | - | - | 140 | 723 |
| Lumber and bamboo products | 3,945 | 20 | - | - | - | 33 | - | - |
| Paper products and printing | 1,960 | - | 1,960 | 1,960 | 1,760 | 5,400 | 2,609 | 4,620 |
| Chemicals | 14,513 | 24,443 | - | - | - | - | 4,253 | 480 |
| Rubber products | 2,985 | 5,500 | 736 | - | - | - | 701 | 2,850 |
| Non-metallic minerals | 7,266 | 475 | 2,162 | - | 1,537 | - | 1,521 | - |
| Base metals and metal products | 1,718 | 923 | - | 646 | 3,000 | - | 23 | 501 |
| Machinery equipment | 322 | - | 50 | - | - | - | 600 | 645 |
| Electronic and electric appliances | 5,118 | 5,526 | 2,498 | - | 3,642 | 27,633 | 22,644 | 25,317 |
| Trade | 6,546 | 2,173 | 1,150 | 1,576 | 144 | 1,343 | 1,718 | 297 |
| Transportation | - | - | - | - | - | - | - | 196 |
| Banking and insurance | - | - | 1,050 | - | - | - | - | 15,267 |
| Services | 166 | - | 250 | 450 | - | 3,680 | 4,475 | 2,850 |
| Other | 2,756 | 2,781 | 908 | 0 | 480 | 578 | 0 | 2,365 |
| **Total** | **59,260** | **42,105** | **10,764** | **11,632** | **10,563** | **39,263** | **41,334** | **56,911** |

Table 4.6 (continued)

**Table 4.6 (continued)**
**Taiwan's Outward Investment by Industry, 1952–1993**
(in thousands of U.S. dollars)

| | 1987 | 1988 | 1989 | 1990 | 1991 | 1992 | 1993 |
|---|---|---|---|---|---|---|---|
| Food and beverage processing | 5,000 | 1,911 | 51 | 163,653 | 13,827 | 4,000 | 14,379 |
| Textiles | 686 | 3,736 | 37,571 | 50,211 | 52,018 | 77,964 | 86,776 |
| Garments and footwear | 1,192 | - | 19 | 2,734 | 3,070 | 4,442 | 8,560 |
| Leather and fur products | - | 2,120 | - | 947 | 510 | - | 554 |
| Lumber and bamboo products | 214 | 620 | 1,520 | 8,934 | 10,238 | 8,401 | 13,787 |
| Paper products and printing | 2,984 | - | 4,618 | 16,520 | 55,469 | 10,861 | 110,504 |
| Chemicals | 9,109 | 28,421 | 414,935 | 77,927 | 67,401 | 71,048 | 310,344 |
| Rubber products | 8,077 | 5,570 | 40,465 | 11,289 | 42,576 | 26,569 | 91 |
| Non-metallic minerals | 3,992 | 1,019 | 1,296 | 121,844 | 63,269 | 3,600 | 23,846 |
| Base metals and metal products | - | 2,925 | 20,411 | 32,483 | 360,263 | 33,783 | 20,867 |
| Machinery equipment | 750 | 158 | 6,860 | 4,886 | 7,878 | 6,583 | 1,038 |
| Electronic and electric appliances | 39,584 | 39,486 | 121,852 | 423,921 | 209,308 | 131,238 | 104,239 |
| Trade | 4,302 | 15,928 | 10,672 | 61,812 | 84,328 | 141,869 | 296,568 |
| Transportation | - | - | 9,909 | 17,432 | 4,299 | 4,828 | 33,584 |
| Banking and insurance | - | 4,000 | 172,372 | 498,481 | 403,740 | 305,381 | 451,763 |
| Services | 8,981 | 111,630 | 54,426 | 43,238 | 246,580 | 48,408 | 67,053 |
| Other | 17,970 | 1,212 | 34,009 | 15,794 | 31,256 | 8,284 | 116,482 |
| **Total** | **102,751** | **218,736** | **930,986** | **1,552,206** | **1,656,030** | **887,259** | **1,660,435** |

*Source:*   Investment Commission, Ministry of Economic Affairs, Taipei, *Statistics on Outward Investment*, various issues.

**Table 4.7**
**Taiwan's Outward Investment by Destination, 1952–October 1994**
(on Approval Basis)

| | Number of projects | Amount (U.S.$ million) | Rank | Distribution of Taiwan's outward investment |
|---|---|---|---|---|
| Mainland China | 10,605 | $4,405.4 | 1 | 33.8% |
| Hong Kong | 274 | 599.2 | 3 | 4.6 |
| Singapore | 92 | 231.5 | 6 | 1.8 |
| Thailand | 196 | 568.9 | 4 | 4.4 |
| Japan | 75 | 101.7 | 7 | 0.8 |
| United States | 660 | 2,432.8 | 2 | 18.6 |
| Panama | 11 | 106.6 | 8 | 0.8 |
| United Kingdom | 38 | 286.3 | 5 | 2.2 |
| Oceania | 23 | 47.6 | - | 0.4 |
| Other areas | 727 | 4,268.2 | - | 32.7 |
| **Total** | **12,746** | **$13,048.2** | - | |

*Source:*   Investment Commission, Ministry of Economic Affairs, Taipei, *Statistics on Outward Investment, Indirect Mainland Investment,* various issues.

*Note:*   Summed percentages may not total 100 percent due to rounding.

**Table 4.8**
**Intraregional Trade within the Western Pacific, 1970–1992**
(in millions of U.S. dollars)

| Western Pacific | 1970 Amount | % | 1980 Amount | % | 1985 Amount | % | 1990 Amount | % | 1992 Amount | % |
|---|---|---|---|---|---|---|---|---|---|---|
| Japan | 8,836 | 23.13 | 77,141 | 28.39 | 90,881 | 29.54 | 169,949 | 32.50 | 204,785 | 35.73 |
| Korea | 1,313 | 46.58 | 13,965 | 35.09 | 20,808 | 33.88 | 53,981 | 40.03 | 67,810 | 42.81 |
| Taiwan | 1,377 | 46.58 | 14,218 | 35.95 | 18,371 | 36.14 | 55,067 | 45.16 | 76,903 | 50.11 |
| Singapore | 2,120 | 52.80 | 23,848 | 54.98 | 26,628 | 54.24 | 59,823 | 52.64 | 69,866 | 51.50 |
| Hong Kong | 1,654 | 30.52 | 20,006 | 47.48 | 33,977 | 56.73 | 99,585 | 60.49 | 151,686 | 62.44 |
| Thailand | 1,010 | 50.27 | 6,636 | 42.22 | 7,701 | 47.06 | 28,035 | 49.66 | 37,064 | 50.66 |
| Malaysia | 1,482 | 47.88 | 12,960 | 54.63 | 16,882 | 60.85 | 34,372 | 58.58 | 48,327 | 59.93 |
| Indonesia | 1,226 | 58.10 | 21,245 | 64.88 | 17,176 | 59.53 | 29,426 | 61.94 | 36,880 | 65.12 |
| Philippines | 1,021 | 44.94 | 5,824 | 41.49 | 4,546 | 45.16 | 9,280 | 43.96 | 11,940 | 45.20 |
| Australia | 2,847 | 30.57 | 17,789 | 41.99 | 21,455 | 46.41 | 37,380 | 47.47 | 43,441 | 52.19 |
| New Zealand | 673 | 27.27 | 4,529 | 41.57 | 5,283 | 45.11 | 8,954 | 47.15 | 9,406 | 49.44 |
| Mainland China | - | - | 17,800 | 46.79 | 40,232 | 57.60 | 72,187 | 63.44 | 106,950 | 68.18 |
| **Total** | **23,559** | **31.55** | **235,961** | **38.42** | **303,940** | **41.09** | **658,039** | **45.28** | **865,058** | **49.16** |

*Sources:*  International Monetary Fund, *Direction of Trade Statistics Yearbook*, 1969–1975, 1987, 1991, 1993; Department of Statistics, Ministry of Finance, Taipei, *Monthly Statistics of Exports and Imports, Taiwan Area, The Republic of China*, various issues; Korea Foreign Trade Association, Seoul, *Major Statistics of Korean Economy*, various issues.

*Notes:*
Amount = the trade with others in the Western Pacific region.
% = the percentage of the country's total trade.

**Table 4.9**
**Intraregional Trade between ASEAN and Other Western Pacific Countries, 1980–1992**
(in millions of U.S. dollars)

| Country | 1980 Amount | % | 1985 Amount | % | 1990 Amount | % | 1992 Amount | % |
|---|---|---|---|---|---|---|---|---|
| Singapore | 11,890 | 33.20 | 14,979 | 30.51 | 35,366 | 31.19 | 42,309 | 31.18 |
| Thailand | 4,692 | 29.85 | 5,327 | 32.55 | 21,530 | 38.14 | 27,984 | 38.25 |
| Malaysia | 8,287 | 34.93 | 10,178 | 36.69 | 20,369 | 34.71 | 28,324 | 35.12 |
| Indonesia | 17,135 | 52.32 | 14,231 | 49.32 | 26,110 | 54.96 | 30,144 | 53.22 |
| Philippines | 4,943 | 35.20 | 3,258 | 32.37 | 7,550 | 35.76 | 9,953 | 37.67 |
| **Total** | **46,947** | **44.30** | **47,973** | **36.31** | **110,925** | **37.30** | **138,714** | **37.24** |

*Sources:* International Monetary Fund, *Direction of Trade Statistics Yearbook, 1969–1975, 1987, 1991, 1993;* Department of Statistics, Ministry of Finance, Taipei, *Monthly Statistics of Exports and Imports, Taiwan Area, The Republic of China,* various issues; Korea Foreign Trade Association, Seoul, *Major Statistics of Korean Economy,* various issues.

*Notes:*   ASEAN excluding Brunei.
The countries of the Western Pacific are Japan, Korea, Taiwan, Singapore, Hong Kong, Thailand, Malaysia, Indonesia, Philippines, Australia, New Zealand, and mainland China.
Amount = the trade with others in the Western Pacific region.
% = the percentage of the country's total trade.

**Table 4.10**
**Taiwan's Export Trade in the Pacific Region, 1980–1993**
(in millions of U.S. dollars)

| Year | Total in the world | Total in the Pacific region | United States | Japan | NIEs | ASEAN |
|------|------|------|------|------|------|------|
| 1980 | 19,810.6 | 12,145.5 | 6,760.3 | 2,173.4 | 2,362.3 | 849.5 |
|      | (100.0) | (61.3) | (34.1) | (11.0) | (11.9) | (4.3) |
| 1985 | 30,725.7 | 22,864.2 | 14,773.4 | 3,460.9 | 3,678.7 | 951.2 |
|      | (100.0) | (74.4) | (48.1) | (11.3) | (12.0) | (3.1) |
| 1986 | 39,861.5 | 28,982.2 | 19,013.9 | 4,559.8 | 4,203.8 | 1,204.7 |
|      | (100.0) | (72.7) | (47.7) | (11.4) | (10.5) | (3.0) |
| 1987 | 53,678.7 | 38,384.7 | 23,684.8 | 6,986.0 | 6,112.0 | 1,601.9 |
|      | (100.0) | (71.5) | (44.1) | (13.0) | (11.4) | (3.0) |
| 1988 | 61,667.4 | 42,864.8 | 23,467.2 | 8,771.7 | 8,187.1 | 2,438.8 |
|      | (100.0) | (69.5) | (38.1) | (14.2) | (13.3) | (4.0) |
| 1989 | 66,304.0 | 46,769.0 | 24,036.2 | 9,064.9 | 10,150.7 | 3,517.2 |
|      | (100.0) | (70.5) | (36.3) | (13.7) | (15.3) | (5.3) |
| 1990 | 67,214.4 | 46,640.7 | 21,745.9 | 8,337.7 | 11,972.7 | 4,584.4 |
|      | (100.0) | (69.4) | (32.4) | (12.4) | (17.8) | (6.8) |
| 1991 | 76,178.3 | 52,596.4 | 22,320.8 | 9,188.9 | 16,121.3 | 4,965.4 |
|      | (100.0) | (69.0) | (29.3) | (12.1) | (21.2) | (6.5) |
| 1992 | 81,470.3 | 57,183.9 | 23,571.6 | 8,893.7 | 19,070.6 | 5,648.0 |
|      | (100.0) | (70.2) | (28.9) | (10.9) | (23.4) | (6.9) |
| 1993 | 84,916.6 | 61,040.8 | 23,484.5 | 8,964.1 | 22,591.8 | 6,000.4 |
|      | (100.0) | (71.9) | (27.7) | (10.6) | (26.6) | (7.1) |

**Table 4.10 (continued)**
**Taiwan's Export Trade in the Pacific Region, 1980–1993**
(in millions of U.S. dollars)

| | NIEs | | | ASEAN (excluding Singapore and Brunei) | | | |
|---|---|---|---|---|---|---|---|
| South Korea | Hong Kong | Singapore | Thailand | Malaysia | Philippines | Indonesia |
| 266.5 | 1,550.6 | 545.2 | 176.3 | 169.9 | 195.0 | 478.2 |
| (1.3) | (7.8) | (2.8) | (0.9) | (0.0) | (1.0) | (2.4) |
| 253.8 | 2,539.7 | 885.2 | 236.2 | 194.9 | 239.2 | 280.9 |
| (0.8) | (8.3) | (2.9) | (0.8) | (0.6) | (0.8) | (0.9) |
| 351.6 | 2,921.3 | 930.9 | 278.6 | 205.7 | 328.6 | 391.8 |
| (0.9) | (7.3) | (2.3) | (0.7) | (0.5) | (0.8) | (1.0) |
| 638.2 | 4,123.3 | 1,350.5 | 424.6 | 272.1 | 459.7 | 445.5 |
| (1.2) | (7.7) | (2.5) | (0.8) | (0.5) | (0.9) | (0.8) |
| 917.3 | 5,587.1 | 1,682.7 | 753.7 | 451.1 | 601.4 | 632.6 |
| (1.5) | (9.1) | (2.7) | (1.2) | (0.7) | (1.0) | (1.0) |
| 1,132.8 | 7,042.3 | 1,975.6 | 1,110.2 | 694.8 | 778.1 | 934.1 |
| (1.7) | (10.6) | (3.0) | (1.7) | (1.0) | (1.2) | (1.4) |
| 1,212.8 | 8,556.2 | 2,203.7 | 1,423.6 | 1,103.6 | 811.4 | 1,245.8 |
| (1.8) | (12.7) | (3.3) | (2.1) | (1.6) | (1.2) | (1.9) |
| 1,287.3 | 12,430.5 | 2,403.5 | 1,444.9 | 1,464.9 | 848.4 | 1,207.2 |
| (1.7) | (16.3) | (3.2) | (1.9) | (1.9) | (1.1) | (1.6) |
| 1,150.4 | 15,415.0 | 2,505.2 | 1,809.6 | 1,600.3 | 1,023.3 | 1,214.8 |
| (1.4) | (18.9) | (3.1) | (2.2) | (2.0) | (1.3) | (1.5) |
| 1,271.5 | 18,444.3 | 2,876.0 | 2,017.1 | 1,668.0 | 1,030.8 | 1,284.5 |
| (1.5) | (21.7) | (3.4) | (2.4) | (2.0) | (1.2) | (1.5) |

*Source:* Ministry of Finance, Taipei, *Monthly Statistics of Exports and Imports, Taiwan Area, The Republic of China*, various issues.

*Note:* Figures in parentheses denote percentage share of Taiwan's total exports in the world.

## 4.11
## Taiwan's Import Trade in the Pacific Region, 1980–1993
(in millions of U.S. dollars and percentages)

| Year | Total in the world | Total in the Pacific region | United States | Japan | NIEs | ASEAN |
|------|---------|---------|---------|---------|---------|---------|
| 1980 | 19,733.1 | 11,878.5 | 4,673.5 | 5,353.2 | 680.1 | 1,171.7 |
|      | (100.0) | (60.2) | (23.7) | (27.1) | (3.4) | (5.9) |
| 1985 | 20,102.0 | 12,223.7 | 4,746.3 | 5,548.8 | 782.2 | 1,146.4 |
|      | (100.0) | (60.8) | (23.6) | (27.6) | (3.9) | (5.7) |
| 1986 | 24,181.5 | 15,908.2 | 5,432.6 | 8,254.7 | 1,047.3 | 1,173.6 |
|      | (100.0) | (65.8) | (22.5) | (34.1) | (4.3) | (4.9) |
| 1987 | 34,983.4 | 22,988.2 | 7,648.0 | 11,840.6 | 1,808.6 | 1,691.0 |
|      | 100.0) | (65.7) | (21.9) | (33.8) | (5.2) | (4.8) |
| 1988 | 49,672.8 | 33,535.4 | 13,006.7 | 14,825.4 | 3,562.3 | 2,141.0 |
|      | (100.0) | (67.5) | (26.2) | (29.8) | 7.2 | (4.3) |
| 1989 | 52,265.3 | 34,589.8 | 12,002.8 | 16,031.0 | 4,333.6 | 2,222.4 |
|      | (100.0) | (66.2) | (23.0) | (30.7) | (8.3) | (4.3) |
| 1990 | 54,716.0 | 35,414.6 | 12,611.8 | 15,998.4 | 4,195.5 | 2,608.9 |
|      | (100.0) | (64.7) | (23.0) | (29.2) | (7.7) | (4.8) |
| 1991 | 62,862.5 | 41,576.9 | 14,113.8 | 18,858.3 | 5,139.7 | 3,465.1 |
|      | (100.0) | (66.1) | (22.5) | (30.0) | (8.2) | (5.5) |
| 1992 | 72,007.0 | 47,681.1 | 15,771.0 | 21,766.6 | 5,777.2 | 4,366.3 |
|      | (100.0) | (66.2) | (21.9) | (30.2) | (8.0) | (6.1) |
| 1993 | 77,061.2 | 50,941.2 | 16,722.6 | 23,186.1 | 6,131.8 | 4,900.7 |
|      | (100.0) | (66.1) | (21.7) | (30.1) | (8.0) | (6.4) |

## 4.11 (continued)
## Taiwan's Import Trade in the Pacific Region, 1980–1993
(in millions of U.S. dollars and percentages)

| NIEs | | | ASEAN (excluding Singapore and Brunei) | | | |
|---|---|---|---|---|---|---|
| South Korea | Hong Kong | Singapore | Thailand | Malaysia | Philippines | Indonesia |
| 208.5 | 249.9 | 221.7 | 89.9 | 424.9 | 117.3 | 539.6 |
| (1.1) | (1.3) | (1.1) | (0.5) | (2.2) | (0.6) | (2.7) |
| 186.6 | 319.7 | 275.9 | 146.9 | 481.5 | 104.2 | 413.8 |
| (0.9) | (1.6) | (1.4) | (0.7) | (2.4) | (0.5) | (2.1) |
| 328.7 | 378.7 | 339.9 | 162.9 | 500.7 | 152.7 | 357.3 |
| (1.4) | (1.6) | (1.4) | (0.7) | (2.1) | (0.6) | (1.5) |
| 532.7 | 753.8 | 522.1 | 200.4 | 729.0 | 194.4 | 567.2 |
| (1.5) | (2.2) | (1.5) | (0.6) | (2.1) | (0.6) | (1.6) |
| 900.1 | 1,922.1 | 740.1 | 341.9 | 943.4 | 242.3 | 613.4 |
| (1.8) | (3.9) | (1.5) | (0.7) | (1.9) | (0.5) | (1.2) |
| 1,239.0 | 2,205.2 | 889.4 | 390.2 | 887.5 | 238.5 | 706.2 |
| (2.4) | (4.2) | (1.7) | (0.7) | (1.7) | (0.5) | (1.4) |
| 1,343.6 | 1,445.9 | 1,406.0 | 448.0 | 1,003.0 | 236.3 | 921.6 |
| (2.5) | (2.6) | (2.6) | (0.8) | (1.8) | (0.4) | (1.7) |
| 1,747.0 | 1,946.8 | 1,445.9 | 586.1 | 1,409.4 | 235.3 | 1,234.3 |
| (2.8) | (3.1) | (2.3) | (0.9) | (2.2) | (0.4) | (2.0) |
| 2,300.9 | 1,781.4 | 1,694.9 | 824.6 | 1,829.2 | 305.2 | 1,407.3 |
| (3.2) | (2.5) | (2.4) | (1.1) | (2.5) | (0.4) | (2.0) |
| 2,537.3 | 1,728.6 | 1,865.9 | 973.0 | 1,938.9 | 364.8 | 1,624.0 |
| (3.3) | (2.2) | (2.4) | (1.3) | (2.5) | (0.5) | (2.1) |

*Source:* Ministry of Finance, Taipei, *Monthly Statistics of Exports and Imports, Taiwan Area, The Republic of China*, various issues.

*Note:* Figures in parentheses denote percentage share of Taiwan's total imports in the world.

**Table 4.12**
**Taiwan's Trade with ASEAN and Mainland China, 1987–1993**
(in millions of U.S. dollars)

| Year | Thailand | | Malaysia | | Philippines | | Indonesia | | Mainland China[a] | |
|---|---|---|---|---|---|---|---|---|---|---|
| | Export | Import | Export | Import | Export | Import | Export | Import | Export | Import |
| 1987 | 424.6 | 200.4 | 272.1 | 729.0 | 459.7 | 194.4 | 445.5 | 567.2 | 1,226.5 | 288.9 |
| 1988 | 753.7 | 341.9 | 451.1 | 943.4 | 601.4 | 242.3 | 632.6 | 613.4 | 2,242.2 | 478.7 |
| 1989 | 1,110.2 | 390.2 | 694.8 | 887.5 | 778.1 | 238.5 | 934.1 | 706.2 | 3,331.9 | 586.9 |
| 1990 | 1,423.6 | 448.0 | 1,103.6 | 1,003.0 | 811.4 | 236.3 | 1,245.8 | 921.6 | 4,394.6 | 765.4 |
| 1991 | 1,444.9 | 586.1 | 1,464.9 | 1,409.4 | 848.0 | 235.3 | 1,207.2 | 1,234.3 | 7,493.5 | 1,125.9 |
| 1992 | 1,809.6 | 824.6 | 1,600.3 | 1,829.2 | 1,023.3 | 305.2 | 1,214.8 | 1,407.3 | 10,547.6 | 1,119.0 |
| 1993 | 2,017.1 | 973.0 | 1,668.0 | 1,938.9 | 1,030.8 | 364.8 | 1,284.5 | 1,624.0 | 13,993.1 | 1,103.6 |

*Source:* Ministry of Finance, Taipei, *Monthly Statistics of Exports and Imports, Taiwan Area, The Republic of China*, various issues; Mainland Affairs Council, Taipei, *Monthly Statistics of Cross-Strait Economic Activities*, various issues.

*Note:* ASEAN excluding Singapore and Brunei.

[a] Refers to indirect trade through Hong Kong. Export data are adjusted by the Mainland Affairs Council according to both Hong Kong and Taiwan customs.

**Table 4.13**
**Taiwans Capital Good Exports to ASEAN, 1981–1991**
(in percentages)

| | Machinery and transportation equipment[a] | | | | | Manufactures[b] | | | | |
|---|---|---|---|---|---|---|---|---|---|---|
| | 1981 | 1985 | 1988 | 1990 | 1991 | 1981 | 1985 | 1988 | 1990 | 1991 |
| Singapore | 32.12 | 25.76 | 47.16 | 51.96 | 51.86 | 88.97 | 85.10 | 94.83 | 96.82 | 95.86 |
| Malaysia | 32.45 | 35.47 | 49.93 | 54.76 | 52.78 | 91.44 | 89.50 | 95.20 | 97.23 | 97.38 |
| Thailand | 40.80 | 26.55 | 41.24 | 43.41 | 45.04 | 89.09 | 72.68 | 91.18 | 91.57 | 93.09 |
| Indonesia | 40.53 | 38.51 | 41.87 | 45.71 | 45.25 | 80.73 | 82.12 | 85.43 | 92.33 | 93.13 |
| Philippines | 18.50 | 14.70 | 26.74 | 26.00 | 26.55 | 71.63 | 86.81 | 89.64 | 93.33 | 93.60 |
| Weighted average[c] | 33.01 | 27.40 | 42.59 | 43.39 | 46.72 | 84.32 | 83.74 | 92.00 | 94.55 | 94.91 |

*Source:* Council for Economic Planning and Development, "Bilateral Relations between Taiwan and ASEAN," internal report, Taipei, 1992 (in Chinese).

*Note:* ASEAN excluding Brunei.

[a] SITC code 7.
[b] SITC codes 5,6,7,8.
[c] Figures represent ratios of Taiwan's exports of listed products to ASEAN (excluding Brunei) over Taiwan's total exports to ASEAN.

**Table 4.14**
**Coefficient of Intra-Industry (Manufacturing) Trade between Taiwan and ASEAN, 1981–1991**
(in percentages)

| SITC | Item | 1981 | 1985 | 1988 | 1990 | 1991 |
|------|------|------|------|------|------|------|
| 5 | Chemicals | 25.39 | 34.72 | 45.15 | 43.33 | 47.82 |
| 6 | Manufactures (classified by raw materials) | 10.85 | 10.75 | 20.57 | 19.66 | 24.01 |
| 7 | Machinery and transportation equipment | 29.18 | 28.55 | 35.34 | 42.51 | 41.47 |
| 8 | Miscellaneous products | 21.28 | 8.86 | 29.95 | 29.23 | 35.10 |
| 5-8 | Manufacturing | 20.87 | 19.68 | 30.71 | 34.40 | 36.47 |

*Source:*   Ministry of Finance, Taipei, *Monthly Statistics of Exports and Imports, Taiwan Area, ROC,* various issues.

*Notes:*   ASEAN excluding Brunei.
        The coefficient is defined as the ratio of an industry's intra-industry trade to the industry's total trade.

**4.15**
**Royalty Proceeds, 1986–1993**
(in millions of U.S. dollars)

| | 1986 | 1987 | 1988 | 1989 | 1990 | 1991 | 1992 | 1993 |
|---|---|---|---|---|---|---|---|---|
| (Intellectual) Property Income: Credit | 4 | 33 | 64 | 85 | 121 | 219 | 322 | 332 |
| (Intellectual) Property Income: Debit | -172 | -274 | -381 | -476 | -582 | -894 | -1,016 | -861 |

*Source:* Central Bank of China, *Balance of Payments, Taiwan District,* Taipei, 1994.

**Table 4.16**
**Outbound Departures of Taiwan Nationals by Destination and Purpose, 1981–1993**

| Destination | Pleasure/Visiting Relatives | | | | Business/Conference | | | |
|---|---|---|---|---|---|---|---|---|
| | 1981 | 1985 | 1990 | 1993 | 1981 | 1985 | 1990 | 1993 |
| **Asia** | 286,702 | 303,125 | 1,919,248 | 3,652,997 | 151,458 | 182,634 | 330,686 | 289,221 |
| Hong Kong | 24,480 | 26,685 | 908,585 | 1,709,737 | 31,792 | 45,222 | 151,813 | 166,031 |
| Japan | 129,240 | 155,635 | 413,446 | 661,864 | 73,244 | 88,869 | 77,243 | 39,159 |
| South Korea | 84,111 | 57,125 | 163,306 | 118,675 | 11,226 | 12,971 | 18,649 | 7,370 |
| ASEAN | 48,215 | 62,730 | 431,362 | 1,099,986 | 27,367 | 31,143 | 82,437 | 68,083 |
| **North America** | 30,129 | 54,526 | 145,958 | 345,945 | 31,283 | 37,266 | 32,711 | 28,044 |
| U.S.A. | 28,987 | 53,201 | 144,420 | 296,725 | 29,066 | 35,492 | 32,495 | 26,369 |
| Canada | 631 | 723 | 1,406 | 37,706 | 724 | 538 | 179 | 1,577 |
| **Europe** | 1,861 | 8,373 | 11,419 | 37,783 | 3,214 | 4,894 | 2,775 | 4,572 |
| **Oceania** | 240 | 716 | 254 | 76,442 | 1,292 | 1,174 | 74 | 4,294 |
| Australia | 229 | 644 | 222 | 65,665 | 913 | 493 | 67 | 3,748 |
| New Zealand | 7 | 15 | 32 | 10,672 | 111 | 100 | 7 | 532 |
| **Africa** | 533 | 485 | 7,860 | 14,114 | 4,268 | 1,231 | 2,144 | 762 |
| **Total** | 319,465 | 367,225 | 2,084,739 | 4,127,281 | 191,515 | 227,199 | 368,390 | 326,893 |

**Table 4.16 (continued)**
**Outbound Departures of Taiwan Nationals by Destination and Purpose, 1981–1993**

| Destination | Other | | | | Total | | | |
|---|---|---|---|---|---|---|---|---|
| | 1981 | 1985 | 1990 | 1993 | 1981 | 1985 | 1990 | 1993 |
| **Asia** | 42,513 | 163,825 | 419,611 | 147,424 | 480,673 | 649,584 | 2,669,545 | 4,089,642 |
| Hong Kong | 16,146 | 46,498 | 185,366 | 59,063 | 72,418 | 118,405 | 1,245,764 | 1,934,831 |
| Japan | 16,002 | 67,669 | 100,446 | 36,077 | 218,486 | 312,173 | 591,135 | 737,100 |
| South Korea | 2,904 | 20,176 | 39,499 | 5,347 | 98,241 | 90,272 | 221,454 | 131,392 |
| ASEAN | 6,487 | 26,039 | 93,491 | 45,863 | 82,069 | 119,912 | 607,290 | 1,213,932 |
| **North America** | 19,489 | 81,396 | 62,850 | 41,037 | 80,901 | 173,188 | 241,519 | 415,026 |
| U.S.A. | 18,346 | 75,468 | 62,410 | 48,656 | 76,399 | 164,161 | 239,325 | 371,750 |
| Canada | 386 | 1,886 | 301 | 4,109 | 1,741 | 3,147 | 1,886 | 43,392 |
| **Europe** | 1,702 | 5,029 | 3,675 | 4,037 | 6,777 | 18,296 | 17,869 | 46,392 |
| **Oceania** | 247 | 845 | 100 | 5,761 | 1,779 | 2,735 | 428 | 86,497 |
| Australia | 226 | 696 | 91 | 4,838 | 1,368 | 1,833 | 380 | 74,251 |
| New Zealand | 5 | 39 | 8 | 918 | 123 | 154 | 47 | 12,122 |
| **Africa** | 606 | 1,270 | 2,951 | 1,005 | 5,407 | 2,986 | 12,955 | 15,881 |
| **Total** | 64,557 | 252,365 | 489,187 | 200,262 | 575,537 | 846,789 | 2,942,316 | 4,654,436 |

*Source:* Tourism Bureau, Ministry of Transportation and Communications, *Annual Report on Tourism Statistics of Transportation and Communications,* Taipei, various issues.

**Table 5.1**
**Indirect Trade between Taiwan and Mainland China through Hong Kong, 1979–1993**
(in millions of U.S. dollars)

| Year | Exports to Mainland China | | | Imports from Mainland China | | Trade total | Trade balance |
| | Hong Kong customs | MAC estimates | % change | $ amount | % change | $ amount | $ amount |
|---|---|---|---|---|---|---|---|
| 1979 | 21.47 | – | – | 56.29 | – | – | – |
| 1980 | 234.97 | – | – | 76.21 | 35.39 | – | – |
| 1981 | 384.15 | 384.8 | – | 75.18 | (1.35) | 459.98 | 309.62 |
| 1982 | 194.45 | 194.5 | (49.45) | 84.02 | 11.76 | 278.52 | 110.48 |
| 1983 | 157.84 | 201.4 | 3.55 | 89.85 | 6.94 | 291.25 | 111.55 |
| 1984 | 425.45 | 425.5 | 111.27 | 127.75 | 42.18 | 553.25 | 297.75 |
| 1985 | 986.83 | 986.8 | 131.92 | 115.90 | (9.28) | 1,102.7 | 870.9 |
| 1986 | 811.33 | 811.3 | (17.78) | 144.22 | 24.43 | 955.52 | 667.08 |
| 1987 | 1,226.53 | 1,226.5 | 51.18 | 288.94 | 100.35 | 1,515.44 | 937.56 |
| 1988 | 2,242.22 | 2,242.2 | 82.81 | 478.69 | 65.67 | 2,720.89 | 1,763.51 |
| 1989 | 2,896.49 | 3,331.9 | 48.60 | 586.90 | 22.61 | 3,918.8 | 2,745.00 |
| 1990 | 3,278.26 | 4,394.6 | 31.89 | 765.36 | 30.41 | 5,159.96 | 3,629.24 |
| 1991 | 4,667.15 | 7,493.5 | 70.52 | 1,125.95 | 47.11 | 8,619.45 | 6,367.55 |
| 1992 | 6,287.93 | 10,547.6 | 40.76 | 1,118.97 | (0.62) | 11,666.57 | 9,428.63 |
| 1993 | 7,585.42 | 13,993.1 | 32.67 | 1,103.56 | (1.38) | 15,096.66 | 12,889.54 |

*Source:* Mainland Affairs Council (MAC), Taipei, *Monthly Statistics of Cross-Strait Economic Activities*, various issues (in Chinese).

**Table 5.2**
**Cross-Strait (Indirect) Trade Interdependence, 1979–1993**
(in percentages)

| Year | Taiwan's Dependence on Mainland China | | | Mainland China's Dependence on Taiwan | | |
|---|---|---|---|---|---|---|
| | Export | Import | Two-way trade | Export | Import | Two-way trade |
| 1979 | 0.13* | 0.38 | 0.25* | 0.41 | 0.14* | 0.27* |
| 1980 | 1.19* | 0.39 | 0.79* | 0.42 | 1.17* | 0.82* |
| 1981 | 1.70 | 0.35 | 1.05 | 0.34 | 1.74 | 1.04 |
| 1982 | 0.88 | 0.44 | 0.68 | 0.38 | 1.01 | 0.67 |
| 1983 | 0.80 | 0.44 | 0.64 | 0.40 | 0.94 | 0.67 |
| 1984 | 1.40 | 0.58 | 1.06 | 0.49 | 1.55 | 1.03 |
| 1985 | 3.21 | 0.58 | 2.17 | 0.42 | 2.34 | 1.58 |
| 1986 | 2.04 | 0.60 | 1.49 | 0.46 | 1.89 | 1.29 |
| 1987 | 2.28 | 0.83 | 1.92 | 0.73 | 2.84 | 1.83 |
| 1988 | 3.70 | 0.96 | 2.47 | 1.01 | 4.06 | 2.65 |
| 1989 | 6.03 | 1.22 | 3.31 | 1.12 | 5.64 | 3.51 |
| 1990 | 6.54 | 1.40 | 4.23 | 1.23 | 8.23 | 4.47 |
| 1991 | 9.84 | 1.79 | 6.20 | 1.57 | 11.75 | 6.35 |
| 1992 | 12.95 | 1.55 | 7.60 | 1.32 | 13.08 | 7.04 |
| 1993 | 16.47 | 1.43 | 9.32 | 1.20 | 13.47 | 7.71 |

*Source:* Mainland Affairs Council, Taipei, *Monthly Statistics of Cross-Strait Economic Activities,* various issues (in Chinese).

* Based on Hong Kong customs data only. Data for 1981 and after are adjusted by the Mainland Affairs Council according to both Hong Kong and Taiwan customs.

**Table 5.3**
**Exports by Taiwan and Mainland China to the United States, 1982–1992**
(in millions of U.S. dollars)

| Year | Mainland China's exports to the U.S. (1) | % annual change | % share of U.S. imports | Taiwan's exports to the U.S. (2) | % annual change | % share of U.S. imports | Ratio: Taiwan's U.S. exports to mainland China's U.S. exports (2)/(1) |
|---|---|---|---|---|---|---|---|
| 1982 | 2,283 | 21.0 | 0.94 | 8,893 | 10.5 | 3.67 | 3.90 |
| 1983 | 2,245 | (1.7) | 0.88 | 11,205 | 26.0 | 4.37 | 4.99 |
| 1984 | 3,064 | 36.5 | 0.95 | 14,765 | 31.8 | 4.57 | 4.82 |
| 1985 | 3,860 | 26.0 | 1.12 | 16,396 | 11.0 | 4.77 | 4.25 |
| 1986 | 4,771 | 23.6 | 1.29 | 19,791 | 20.7 | 5.37 | 4.15 |
| 1987 | 6,194 | 31.9 | 1.54 | 24,622 | 24.4 | 6.12 | 3.91 |
| 1988 | 8,512 | 35.2 | 1.95 | 24,804 | 0.7 | 5.67 | 2.91 |
| 1989 | 11,988 | 40.8 | 2.56 | 24,326 | (1.9) | 5.20 | 2.03 |
| 1990 | 15,224 | 27.0 | 3.10 | 22,667 | (6.8) | 4.62 | 1.49 |
| 1991 | 18,855 | 23.9 | 3.90 | 22,941 | 1.2 | 4.75 | 1.22 |
| 1992 | 25,514 | 35.3 | 4.87 | 24,530 | 6.9 | 4.68 | 0.96 |

*Source:* Board of Foreign Trade, Ministry of Economic Affairs, Taipei, *Press Release*, no. 235, August 1993 (in Chinese).

**Table 5.4**

**Exports by Taiwan and Mainland China to Japan, 1982–1992**

(in millions of U.S. dollars)

| Year | Mainland China's exports to Japan (1) | % annual change | % share of Japan's imports | Taiwan's exports to Japan (2) | % annual change | % share of Japanese imports | Ratio: Taiwan's Japan exports to mainland China's Japan exports (2) / (1) |
|------|------|------|------|------|------|------|------|
| 1982 | 5,352 | – | 4.06 | 2,243 | – | 1.85 | 0.46 |
| 1983 | 5,087 | (4.95) | 4.02 | 2,618 | 16.72 | 2.07 | 0.51 |
| 1984 | 5,979 | 17.53 | 4.37 | 3,214 | 22.77 | 2.35 | 0.54 |
| 1985 | 6,484 | 8.45 | 5.01 | 3,387 | 5.38 | 2.62 | 0.52 |
| 1986 | 5,679 | (12.42) | 4.49 | 4,689 | 38.44 | 3.71 | 0.83 |
| 1987 | 7,422 | 30.69 | 4.95 | 7,150 | 52.48 | 4.77 | 0.96 |
| 1988 | 9,865 | 32.92 | 5.26 | 8,749 | 22.36 | 4.67 | 0.89 |
| 1989 | 11,146 | 12.99 | 5.29 | 8,979 | 2.63 | 4.26 | 0.81 |
| 1990 | 12,011 | 7.76 | 5.13 | 8,471 | (5.66) | 3.62 | 0.71 |
| 1991 | 14,216 | 18.36 | 6.01 | 9,493 | 12.06 | 4.01 | 0.67 |
| 1992 | 16,953 | 19.25 | 7.28 | 9,449 | (0.46) | 4.06 | 0.56 |

*Source:* Board of Foreign Trade, Ministry of Economic Affairs, Taipei, *Press Release*, no. 235, August 1993 (in Chinese).

**Table 5.5**

**Foreign Direct Investment in Mainland China by Source, 1991–September 1993 (Contract Basis)**

(in millions of U.S. dollars)

| Country or Area | 1991 | | | 1992 | | | January-September 1993 | | |
|---|---|---|---|---|---|---|---|---|---|
| | No. of projects | $ | % of total $ | No. of projects | $ | % of total $ | No. of projects | $ | % of total $ |
| Hong Kong | 8,879 | $8,073.59 | 41.23 | 31,892 | $42,695.95 | 61.49 | 39,668 | $59,213.24 | 63.76 |
| Taiwan | 1,735 | 1,392.34 | 7.11 | 6,430 | 5,547.90 | 7.99 | 8,360 | 7,905.67 | 8.51 |
| Japan | 607 | 2,276.44 | 11.62 | 1,809 | 3,323.75 | 4.79 | 2,577 | 4,343.50 | 4.68 |
| United States | 694 | 575.02 | 2.94 | 3,265 | 3,170.85 | 4.57 | 5,060 | 4,965.64 | 5.35 |
| Germany | 27 | 616.50 | 3.15 | 133 | 49.0 | 0.07 | 245 | 553.72 | 0.60 |
| Singapore | 169 | 165.21 | 0.84 | 742 | 1,007.27 | 1.45 | 1,240 | 2,009.75 | 2.16 |
| South Korea | 6 | 1.28 | 0.007 | 650 | 420.54 | 0.61 | 1,210 | 878.62 | 0.95 |
| Other | 969 | 6,482.22 | 33.10 | 3,937 | 13,223.47 | 19.04 | 5,779 | 13,001.55 | 14.00 |
| **Total** | **13,086** | **$19,582.60** | **100.00** | **48,858** | **$69,438.73** | **100.00** | **64,139** | **$92,871.69** | **100.01** |

*Source:* Mainland Affairs Council, Taipei, *Monthly Statistics of Cross-Strait Economic Activities*, various issues (in Chinese).

**Table 5.6**
**Taiwan's Share of Foreign Direct Investment in Mainland China, 1988–September 1993**
(in billions of U.S. dollars)

| Year | Contract Basis | | | | Actual Basis | | | |
|---|---|---|---|---|---|---|---|---|
| | Total foreign investment in mainland China | Investment by Taiwan | Taiwan's share (%) | Rank | Total foreign investment in mainland China | Investment by Taiwan | Taiwan's share (%) | Rank |
| up to 1988 | $75.8 | $6.2 | – | – | $29.6 | $– | – | – |
| 1989 | 11.5 | 0.6 | 4.79 | – | 10.1 | – | – | – |
| 1990 | 12.1 | 0.9 | 7.28 | – | 10.3 | 0.2 | 2.14 | – |
| 1991 | 19.6 | 1.4 | 7.11 | 3 | 11.6 | 0.5 | 4.07 | 3 |
| 1992 | 69.4 | 5.5 | 7.99 | 2 | 19.2 | 1.1 | 5.47 | 3 |
| 1993 (Jan–Sept) | 92.9 | 7.9 | 8.51 | 2 | 22.6 | 1.9 | 8.2 | 3 |
| **1979–Sept 1993** | **$284.0** | **$16.9** | **5.95** | **2** | **$103.3** | **$3.8** | **3.7** | **3** |

*Source:* Mainland Affairs Council, Taipei, *Monthly Statistics of Cross-Strait Economic Activities*, various issues (in Chinese).

**Table 5.7**
**Taiwan's Investment in Mainland China by Industry, 1991–October 1994**
(in millions of U.S. dollars)

| Industry | 1991–1993 | | | January–October 1994 | | |
|---|---|---|---|---|---|---|
| | No. of projects | Amount | % of total amount | No. of projects | Amount | % of total amount |
| Electronic and electrical products | 1,267 | $511.23 | 14.24 | 128 | 141.06 | 17.29 |
| Plastics | 1,088 | 439.23 | 12.24 | 74 | 66.30 | 8.13 |
| Food and beverage | 840 | 388.86 | 10.83 | 70 | 133.13 | 16.32 |
| Precision instruments | 1,225 | 311.26 | 8.67 | 73 | 42.00 | 5.15 |
| Base metal products | 800 | 273.90 | 7.63 | 68 | 77.20 | 9.46 |
| Textiles | 503 | 223.98 | 6.24 | 33 | 32.44 | 3.98 |
| Chemicals | 634 | 205.37 | 5.72 | 67 | 48.91 | 5.99 |
| Non-metallic and mineral products | 429 | 191.93 | 5.35 | 31 | 71.41 | 8.75 |
| Lumber and bamboo products | 438 | 158.79 | 4.42 | 35 | 21.49 | 2.63 |
| Rubber products | 184 | 158.40 | 4.41 | 15 | 21.42 | 2.63 |
| Other | 2,422 | 726.63 | 20.24 | 226 | 160.49 | 19.67 |
| **Total** | **9,830** | **$3,589.56** | **100.00** | **820** | **$815.85** | **100.00** |

**Table 5.7 (continued)**

**Taiwan's Investment in Mainland China by Industry, 1991–October 1994**

(in millions of U.S. dollars)

| Industry | 1991–October 1994 | | | |
|---|---|---|---|---|
| | No. of projects | Amount | % of total amount | Average $ per project (thousands) |
| Electronic and electrical products | 1,395 | $652.28 | 14.81 | $467.58 |
| Plastics | 1,162 | 505.52 | 11.47 | 435.04 |
| Food and beverage | 910 | 521.99 | 11.85 | 573.62 |
| Precision instruments | 1298 | 353.26 | 8.02 | 272.16 |
| Base metal products | 868 | 351.11 | 7.97 | 404.50 |
| Textiles | 536 | 256.44 | 5.82 | 478.43 |
| Chemicals | 701 | 254.27 | 5.77 | 362.72 |
| Non-metallic and mineral products | 460 | 263.33 | 5.98 | 572.46 |
| Lumber and bamboo products | 473 | 180.28 | 4.09 | 381.14 |
| Rubber products | 199 | 179.81 | 4.08 | 903.57 |
| Other | 2,648 | 887.12 | 20.14 | 335.02 |
| **Total** | **10,650** | **$4,405.41** | **100.00** | **$413.65** |

*Source:* Mainland Affairs Council, Taipei, *Monthly Statistics of Cross-Strait Economic Actitities,* various issues (in Chinese).

**Table 5.8**

**Geographical Distribution of Taiwan's Investment in Mainland China, 1991–October 1994**
(in millions of U.S. dollars)

| Area | 1991–1993 | | | January–October 1994 | | |
|---|---|---|---|---|---|---|
| | No. of projects | Amount | % of total amount | No. of projects | Amount | % of total amount |
| Guangdong[a] | 1,260 | $462.17 | 12.88 | 74 | $66.69 | 8.17 |
| Shanghai | 1,083 | 449.12 | 12.51 | 123 | 131.42 | 16.11 |
| Jiangsu[b] | 816 | 444.39 | 12.38 | 106 | 199.14 | 24.41 |
| Shenzhen | 831 | 315.38 | 8.79 | 47 | 28.47 | 3.49 |
| Dongguan | 684 | 262.87 | 7.32 | 55 | 40.61 | 4.98 |
| Xiamen | 544 | 231.42 | 6.45 | 29 | 41.20 | 5.05 |
| Fujian[c] | 749 | 220.44 | 6.14 | 43 | 26.77 | 3.28 |
| Guangzhou | 419 | 154.71 | 4.13 | 31 | 46.02 | 5.64 |
| Zhejiang | 498 | 139.99 | 3.90 | 53 | 48.85 | 5.99 |
| Fuzhou | 339 | 104.89 | 2.92 | 19 | 17.25 | 2.11 |
| Other | 2,607 | 804.17 | 22.40 | 240 | 169.42 | 20.77 |
| **Total** | **9,830** | **$3,589.56** | **100.00** | **820** | **$815.84** | **100.00** |

**Table 5.8 (continued)**
**Geographical Distribution of Taiwan's Investment in Mainland China, 1991–October 1994**
(in millions of U.S. dollars)

| Area | 1991–October 1994 | | | |
| --- | --- | --- | --- | --- |
| | No. of projects | Amount | % of total amount | Average $ per project (thousands) |
| Guangdong[a] | 1,334 | $528.86 | 12.00 | $396.45 |
| Shanghai | 1,206 | 580.54 | 13.18 | 481.38 |
| Jiangsu[b] | 922 | 643.54 | 14.61 | 697.98 |
| Shenzhen | 878 | 343.86 | 7.81 | 391.64 |
| Dongguan | 739 | 303.48 | 6.89 | 410.66 |
| Xiamen | 573 | 272.62 | 6.19 | 475.78 |
| Fujian[c] | 792 | 247.21 | 5.61 | 312.13 |
| Guangzhou | 450 | 200.73 | 4.56 | 446.07 |
| Zhejiang | 551 | 188.85 | 4.29 | 342.74 |
| Fuzhou | 358 | 122.15 | 2.77 | 341.20 |
| Other | 2,847 | 973.59 | 22.10 | 341.97 |
| **Total** | **10,650** | **$4,405.43** | **100.00** | **$413.66** |

*Source:* Mainland Affairs Council, Taipei, *Monthly Statistics of Cross-Strait Economic Activities,* various issues (in Chinese).
[a] Excluding Shenzhen, Dongguan, and Guangzhou
[b] Excluding Shanghai
[c] Excluding Xiamen and Fuzhou

# About the Editors

A Rhodes scholar with M.Phil. and Ph.D. degrees in international relations from Oxford, GERRIT W. GONG holds the Freeman Chair in China Studies at CSIS and has directed the CSIS Asian Studies Program since 1989. Dr. Gong's government experience includes service in the U.S. State Department as Special Assistant to Under Secretary of State for Political Affairs Michael H. Armacost and Special Assistant to U.S. Ambassadors Winston Lord and James Lilley at the U.S. Embassy in Beijing. He was a fellow in Sino-Soviet Studies at CSIS from 1981 to 1985. He has also served on the faculties of The Johns Hopkins University School of Advanced International Studies and Oxford University. He is author of *The Standard of "Civilization" in International Society* (Clarendon Press, 1984) and has published articles in foreign policy journals in both the United States and Asia, including "A Cross-Strait Summit? Some Observations from Washington," in the January 16, 1995, issue of the *China Times* in Taipei; *The Southeast Asian Boom* with Keith W. Eirinberg; "Defining a New Consensus for U.S. China Policy," in *U.S. China Policy: Building a New Consensus*; and "China's Fourth Revolution," *The Washington Quarterly*, Winter 1994. In May 1994, in testimony before the U.S. Senate Subcommittee on East Asian and Pacific Affairs, Dr. Gong presented "Defining a New Consensus for U.S. China Policy."

As vice president and director of studies at CSIS, ERIK R. PETERSON oversees the development and execution of the Center's broad-based research agenda. He also directs the CSIS publications program, which includes the *Washington Papers* and *Significant Issues* series, and serves as cochairman of the Board of Editors of the Center's quarterly journal, *The Washington Quarterly*. Peterson came to the Center from Kissinger Associates, where he was director of research and head of the firm's Washington, D.C. office. Among his writings are "Looming Collision of Capitalisms?", *The Washington Quarterly,* Spring 1994 and reprinted in Eugene R. Wittkopf (ed.), *The Global Edition* (New York: McGraw-Hill, 1994); "An Agenda for Managing Relations with Russia" and "The Enterprise for the Americas Initiative and a U.S.-Chilean FTA," in Robert E. Hunter and Erik R. Peterson (eds.), *Agenda '93: CSIS Policy Action Papers,* December 1993; *The Gulf Cooperation Council: Search for Unity in a Dynamic Region* (1988); and "The Outlook for the GCC in the Postwar Gulf" in J. E. Peterson, ed., *Saudi Arabia and the Gulf States* (1989). Peterson holds an M.B.A. in finance and international business from the Wharton School of the University of Pennsylvania (1991). He received an M.A. in international law and economics from the Paul H. Nitze School of Advanced International Studies at The Johns Hopkins University and a B.A. in international affairs from Colby College. He also holds the Certificate of Eastern European Studies from the University of Fribourg in Switzerland.

East Asia Economic and Financial Outlook

*Other Books in the Series*

# China's Domestic Economy in Regional Context
*Ding Jingping*

Ding Jingping assesses the explosion in East Asian growth and the role of "greater China" from the standpoint of Beijing. The author analyzes the outlook for continued high growth and economic reform in the People's Republic of China, including the impact of economic reforms on state-owned enterprises and contradictions between economic "openness" and regulating foreign investment. The role of external economic relations in China's economic development, particularly with Taiwan, Hong Kong, the United States, and Japan, is also discussed.

**Contents:**

1. Introduction

2. China's Economic and Financial Status

3. Problems of Economic Development

4. Effects of Economic Reform on State-Owned Enterprises

5. Attracting and Utilizing Foreign Capital

6. China's Economic and Foreign Relations

7. The Future of China's Economy

DING JINGPING is senior research fellow and deputy director of the Foreign Affairs Bureau of the Chinese Academy of Social Sciences in Beijing.

*Significant Issues Series*   1995
ISBN 0-89206-318-1   $14.95

❖   ❖   ❖

# Hong Kong's Economic and Financial Future
*Y. F. Luk*

This volume in the East Asia Economic and Financial Outlook series assesses Hong Kong's phenomenal economic performance of the last few decades and, in particular, its special relationship with the People's Republic of China. The author also examines the changing domestic economic policies and political institutions that have played crucial roles in Hong Kong's growth and asks whether this spectacular growth will continue into the next decade.

**Contents:**

1. The Hong Kong Economy: Early Development and Salient Features

2. Recent Developments

3. The Outlook for the Hong Kong Economy

4. Conclusion

Y. F. LUK is a lecturer in the School of Economics and Finance at the University of Hong Kong and editor at the Hong Kong Centre for Economic Research.

*Significant Issues Series*   1995
ISBN 0-89206-306-8   $14.95

❖   ❖   ❖

For information on these and other CSIS publications, contact:

**CSISBOOKS**
1800 K Street, N.W.
Washington, D.C.   20006
Telephone     202-775-3119
Facsimile      202-775-3199